Inside the Not So Big House

Inside the Not So Big House

Discovering
the Details
that Bring
a Home to Life

Sarah Susanka
and Marc Vassallo

Photographs by Ken Gutmaker

The Taunton Press

For Jim, who taught me ever so carefully
to pay attention to all the details

 **The Taunton Press**
Inspiration for hands-on living®

The Taunton Press, Inc., 63 South Main Street, PO Box 5506, Newtown, CT 06470-5506
e-mail: tp@taunton.com

Inside the Not So Big House was previously published in 2005 in hardcover by The Taunton Press, Inc.

Editor: Peter Chapman
Cover design: Alexander Isley, Inc.
Interior design/Layout: Carol Petro
Illustrator: Christine Erikson
Photographer: Ken Gutmaker

LIBRARY OF CONGRESS CATALOGING-IN-PUBLICATION DATA
Susanka, Sarah.
 Inside the not so big house : discovering the details that bring a home to life / Sarah Susanka and Marc Vassallo.
   p. cm.
 ISBN 1-56158-681-1 hardcover
 ISBN 978-1-56158-984-5 paperback
1. Interior architecture. 2. Architecture--Details. 3. Room layout (Dwellings) 4. Small houses. I. Vassallo, Marc. II. Title.
 NA2850.S8 2005
 728'.37--dc22
                                    2005008228

Printed in Singapore
10 9 8 7 6 5 4 3 2 1

The following manufacturers/names appearing in *Inside the Not So Big House* are trademarks:
Homasote®, IKEA®, Kirkstone®, VW™

Acknowledgments

from Sarah   This book would not have been possible without the infectious enthusiasm and unusual combination of architectural and editorial skills brought to the table by my friend and colleague Marc Vassallo.

Putting a book together is no small undertaking, and with all the topics I want to cover to put answers into the hands of the homeowners who need them, I knew I could use some help with a number of the titles I have in mind. Marc's background was perfect, and so was born the vision for a book I'd wanted to write for years, but simply hadn't had the time for. And even as we put the finishing touches on *Inside the Not So Big House*, our next one is on the drawing board—a book about small-scale remodelings.

I'll let Marc take it from here in extending our gratitude to all the other players who've made this book possible, but since he's unlikely to sing his own praises, I wanted to let you know that without Marc this book would not have been born for several more years.

from Marc   Everyone at The Taunton Press deserves our gratitude, especially Jim Childs, Maria Taylor, Paula Schlosser, Carol Singer, Maureen Graney, Wendi Mijal, Robyn Doyon Aitken, Katie Benoit, and most of all, Peter Chapman, our steadfast editor.

We'd like to thank our new friend, photographer Ken Gutmaker, and his wife, Linda, for criss-crossing the country to capture the wonderful photographs in this book. Thanks also to the architects whose designs appear here and to the homeowners who graciously shared their homes and a piece of their lives to make this book possible. We also want to acknowledge all the architects and designers who submitted work for our consideration.

At one point or another, virtually my entire family provided me with a place to work or a place to stay during visits to houses. A big thank-you goes to Lori and Barry Rochelle, Susan and Paul Morton, Paul and Jeremy Vassallo, Ted Vassallo, my second parents John and Sylvia Gatzy, and—not least—my mother, Josephine Vassallo. I'd also like to acknowledge my father, Domenic Vassallo, too long gone, who steered me toward architecture through his own love of design.

Thank you Phyllis Wender, my agent, for your good sense and perseverance.

Thanks of course to you, Sarah, my collaborator, for two very big things—your genius and your generosity.

Most of all I want to thank my wife, Linda, and my son, Nicky, for their boundless patience, good humor, and inspiration. Thanks for keeping the home fires burning. From me, this book is for you.

Contents

Preface

I started planning this book just a few months after my first book, *The Not So Big House,* was published in the fall of 1998. So many people had written to me asking how to make their own houses embody the spirit of building Not So Big. Many of them had noticed a level of detail that is absent in most newer homes today.

These readers wanted to know how to create for themselves some of the things they'd observed as they read and looked at the photos—things like the plate rail I'd included in my own St. Paul house, which I described in passing as a built-in detail that served many functions. This plate rail provided a place to exhibit some objects I loved; it housed a light cove; it provided a surface for the continuous maple trim band to wrap around kitchen and dining areas; and in the process of doing all these things, it created a sense of shelter for the activities taking place below. Or the ship's ladder allowing access to the tiny attic at the top of the same house. Several readers had written, wanting to know how to incorporate a similar detail into their own home. How steep was the stair, how wide, and how big were the cutouts for hands to grip properly?

I realized there were a lot of people looking for solutions to personalize their homes and make them more functional who, up until now, hadn't understood that this could be accomplished with features that are literally built in rather than brought to the house after construction (or remodeling) is complete.

The point of a book focusing on this more up-close view of house design was brought home even more clearly for me when one of The Taunton Press editorial staff told me she had completely misunderstood what I was aiming for. She had been mislead by the word "detail," which she explained to me means something akin to accessorizing—the art of decorating, if you will—to most non-architects. By contrast, what I wanted to describe were the special features of house design that are *permanently* attached to the interior and will remain there as the house passes to future owners. If you were able to turn your house upside down and shake it, these INSIDE details are the ones that wouldn't come off.

Through interactions with hundreds of interested homeowners, it has become a lot clearer to me how to explain this more "close up" level of home design. My goal is to help you make a house that, even before any of your belongings are brought in, still expresses something of your inner spirit and passion for life. As expressed by William Blake's famous aphorism, "All the world's in a grain of sand," a home that's designed well at every scale truly reflects its owners, whether you look at it from a distance or observe its smallest detail. The ideas you'll read about in the coming pages will help you build into your home some personal details that delight you daily and allow even the smallest elements to embody the character of the house as a whole.

The Not So Big House Up Close

Attention to the small gives character to the whole.

(Right) The smallest detail, like the way the flutes on the vertical window trim echo the horizontal lines of the top molding, reverberates at the level of the whole room.

Shortly after I started my architectural training

I moved into a house with 15 other architecture students. I learned a lot from my fellow students, but what stands out most is the amazing education I got in how to look at my surroundings. I'd always been interested in architectural design, long before I knew what that was, drawing floor plans of imaginary houses as a child and building elaborate structures with blocks until well into my teens.

I loved visiting buildings of all types, checking out how they affected me spatially. But I'd always looked at the big picture when noting my experiences. I'd ask myself, how does this space make me feel? Does its shape and size please me? Would I want to spend more time here? What would I change? I had been blissfully unaware of the smaller features of the world around me.

The older architecture students helped me to tighten my focus— literally as you do when you zoom in with a camera lens. Instead of looking at a whole room, for example, I began to focus on the way two pieces of molding were brought

together at the side (jamb) and top (head) of the door into the kitchen. I took note of the way each resident of our house had embellished his or her room, attaching intriguingly designed structures to the walls and floors, such as desk alcoves and drawing equipment containers, and even building up into the truss space above to create bed lofts and skylight shafts. Through it all, I got a crash course in what architects call "detailing." And like my fellow students I learned to zoom into this level of focus, no matter where I was.

For most non-architects, this level of reality is as invisible as it was to me before my initiation into the world of details. Although these small touches often go unnoticed, they have a huge effect on our experience of a place. One reason that so many older homes are venerated is because they have this zoomed-in attention to the little things, like the wall inset at the bottom of the stairway shown in the left photo on p. 9. Most people assume it's the building's age that gives it its charm, when in fact it's the attention to the smaller details that makes it feel so good. This example was in fact built only recently, yet it embodies the sensibility of the house it's a part of, adding to its integrity and character while expressing something that's more than skin deep about its owners in the process.

Built-In Character

In my first book, *The Not So Big House*, I made the case that a house isn't really a home unless it is filled with the personality of its inhabitants. But how do you accomplish that? Most homeowners assume this means filling the space you have with things that have meaning to you, and certainly this is an important step in the right direction. But a

(Top) Even if you don't focus on the trim, it helps you make sense of the layers of space in this view from room to room to room. (Above and facing page) The window seat is treated as a little room. As you zoom in, the impact of details like trim, shelving, wide windowsills, and drawers adds up. The result is a space that's small in size but rich in character.

A wall niche with a small statue animates the entry area and serves as a focal point at the base of the stairs.

house that really sings has character that's built in, so that even if the house were completely emptied of furniture and objects collected over a lifetime, the house would still feel warm and inviting. It would still have a character all its own.

Sadly, all too many of the new houses and remodels built today would fail this test. To keep construction costs down, all the money available goes into square footage, leaving little or no money for the special details that can really make a house a beautiful place. The house in the photo on the facing page, on the other hand, would still be beautiful even without its occupants' belongings adorning its various surfaces.

In an effort to remedy this situation, I wrote *The Not So Big House* to help people looking for a more personal home understand what's missing in the average house. I suggested that the key to creating a home with intrinsic character is to keep the overall size down so that you can reapportion some dollars out of square footage and into the details that make the house a delight to live in. Although I've tried where possible in illustrating this book to find details that will not break the bank, they still do add to the cost of a home. A handy rule of thumb is that if you strive to reduce the square footage you were originally planning by about one third, and make available the dollars saved for personalizing your home, you'll have enough money to do the kind of detailing shown here.

In the short hallway shown at left, a lowered ceiling compresses space before releasing it into the taller master bedroom beyond, creating a satisfying sense of arrival.

This wall shelf was built with strips of basic pine lumber, but its elegant composition transcends the ordinariness of its materials.

God Is in the Details

We've all heard the phrase, "God is in the details," made famous by architect Mies van der Rohe in 1959, but what does it really mean? What is a detail anyway? The details you'll see illustrated in this book are *not* what interior designers would call accessories—things like vases, wall hangings, and artwork. To use the analogy I used in the introduction, if you were to turn the house upside down and shake it, all these accessories would fall instantly from their various perches. The details we'll be discussing here are built right into the house, so they're attached permanently and won't fall off. They're designed in from the beginning, to help both personalize the house and make it function more efficiently.

To architects the word *detail* implies the marriage of materials to create design elements or combinations that are built in during the construction (or remodeling) process. The photo above is a classic example of what an architect means by the term. This medicine shelf, suspended above the toilet in a not so big bathroom, involves the interconnection of several wooden elements of different types. First, there is the 1x8 pine cap that stretches from one side of the alcove to the other, hugging the ceiling. Next there are the shelves themselves, made of 1x4 pine

We're drawn naturally to cozy spaces like this eating area, but for such spaces to feel comfortable and function well, all the parts—windowsill, seat back, tabletop—have to be sized just right.

boards. Then there are the pairs of vertical "suspenders," made of narrower pieces of the same wood species. And finally there are the wooden "pegs" between the vertical suspenders, which are made of cherry, to give a contrasting but complementary color.

In combination these four parts are brought together to create something that looks both beautiful and effortless. Yet like all good design, it took someone, in this case North Carolina architect Tina Govan, to conceive and develop the composition, include it as a drawing in the blueprints for the house, and to make sure it was executed in the way she intended by the craftsman who built it. The connection of one part to another is, strictly speaking, a detail, and when all these interconnection are considered together they become one larger detail. So the word itself implies multiple levels of design.

Let's look at a variety of these different levels of detail, so you get a sense for the kinds of information you'll find in the rest of the book.

Details in Context

Most people think of details as a relatively small thing—a doorknob, a newel post, a shelf bracket—but the word *detail* can also refer to larger elements such as window seats and breakfast nooks, hearths and accent walls, built-in cabinets and kitchen islands. Take a look at the two photos on this page and the top left photo on p. 13 and you'll see

The quality and functionality of this narrow entry hall have been improved considerably with the addition of a small but thoughtfully outfitted and proportioned seating alcove.

details at this scale: a bench seat in a Minnesota mudroom flanked by cabinets on either side, and a triptych of windows above, that together create a practical but welcoming informal entryway for a family with young children; an informal eating area with benches and table proportioned just right for the body sizes of the homeowners, with a horizontal band that serves both as windowsill and apron for the window and as backsplash for the table; and a stairway with open risers, its treads spanning from side to side with no visible means of support. For the stairway to look so elegant, the architect or builder had to figure out how to support those treads and hide the fastening system from view. If I hadn't pointed out this particular detail to you, you probably wouldn't have wondered how it was done. Your eye simply accepts it. You may like the way it looks, but to duplicate it you need this information, or someone ingenious enough to create the same look.

The repetition of paint colors helps unite these rooms. Less obvious is the unifying effect of thin lines as a motif for everything from window trim to table legs, chair slats, and picture frames.

Details in Combination

The word *detail* can also be used to describe materials and how they are used: concrete for countertops, hand-rubbed fir for ceiling beams, stainless steel for the stair rails. The top right photo shown on the facing page illustrates the marriage of two materials, wood and slate, interpenetrating to create an intriguing pattern at the same time

Each material in this entry area—slate, oak flooring, and embossed glass—expresses its unique nature in relation to the other materials. At the same time, the natural textures and colors of the materials work together to create a feeling of harmony.

Stair treads with no visible means of support seem to float, adding to the light, buoyant quality of the entire house.

Carrying the band of black tile around the window trim emphasizes the window and gives the small bathroom a unique look.

as they inventively solve the problem of where to stop one surface and start the next one. Obviously, if someone hadn't thought this detail through and drawn out what they were imagining, the chances of it being anything noteworthy would have been slim. But when designed and communicated to the craftspeople involved, the detail becomes an engaging aspect of the home.

*Detail*s can also refer to design elements that are not objects at all, but rather qualities that carry throughout the house, such as a palette of colors, a particular surface texture, or a character of glass that creates a particular quality of light. For example, the colors used in the remodeling shown in the photo on the facing page are carried throughout the house—sage green for trim, pale yellow for walls, and natural hardwood floors—which gives the whole a heightened sense of cohesiveness.

A type of detail that is familiar in older homes is the kind that defines the shape of something, such as the casing or trim that runs around all the doors and windows in a house, or the wainscot that wraps the bottom half of all the rooms on the main level of a home. The photo at left is an example of this type of detail. The black tile serves primarily as a baseboard and beltline, as these two lines define the perimeter of the room. But where the window interrupts the beltline, instead of stopping and starting the line, the black tile band carries

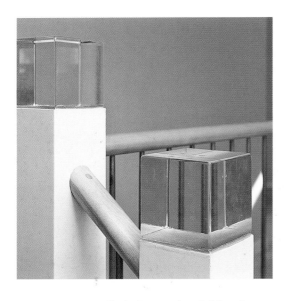

on around the window, giving the room a unique and attractive character in the process.

Details in Focus

The details that can *sometimes* have the biggest impact are very small things indeed, like the wainscot cap we looked at earlier or the newel-post caps shown here. A reinterpretation of the traditional post cap, these are made of glass, and add a delightfully contemporary flair to a simple cottage.

My favorite detail in this category is the horizontal cherry lattice that I've used in a number of houses I've designed over the last few years. I use it both to create a segment of lowered ceiling to separate one space from another, as well as to add some geometrical patterning and visual weight. The effect is engaging, especially at night when the light from recessed cans above filters through the lattice to create fascinating patterns on the floor below. I first saw a detail similar to this one in the old section of Kyoto when I traveled to Japan a few years ago. I was so intrigued by the detail that I started using it in my own work as soon as I returned. My St. Paul house was the first experiment, and ever since then I've been refining both the proportions and the method of construction. Horizontal lattice is a relatively simple detail to build, but one that can have a significant effect on the pleasure you derive from your house.

Details that resolve the meeting of materials are the ones that are almost completely invisible to someone who doesn't know what to look for, and yet they can be the most elegant. The photo shown at right on the facing page will give you an idea of how to train your eye to notice

The lowered ceiling created by a floating lattice panel frames the kitchen beyond, defining it as a place apart from the dining area (in the foreground), while allowing space and light to flow between the rooms.

them. In this tiny master bathroom it was desirable to use every trick in the book to make the room look larger. So the architect brought the mirror all the way to the countertop as well as to the adjacent door jamb. There's not even a C-channel at the edge of the mirror (the little border you find on most mirrors that actually cups its ends so you don't see the edges), so your eye is led to believe that there's no wall there at all. It looks as though there are two sinks directly facing each other, though of course this is an optical illusion. It's the detailing of how the mirror meets the countertop that creates the effect.

Another such detail is the marriage of materials around the window boxes on an interior porch shown in the bottom left photo on p. 16. The vertical wood brackets, made to look like fins, secure perforated steel flower boxes that serve in place of railings. As these same fins extend below the opening, they terminate a few inches short of the flat casing on either side, and a square-head stainless-steel bolt holds the entire assembly in place. This is the kind of detail that, as soon as I see it, I know for certain that an architect has been involved. To make it look this crafted, the architect had to carefully draw all the interrelationships between the various parts, and track down a source for both the square-head bolts and the perforated metal.

Small detail, big impact: a mirror that meets the countertop creates the illusion of more space.

No accidents here. This detail is a labor of love, and though it may seem obsessive for many homeowners it clearly indicates the refinement that's possible when you pay attention to the little details that make a house personal.

What It All Adds Up To

Appreciating details is really just a process of learning to zoom in and focus on what's important at this smaller scale of consideration. Some details are so simple they're hardly noticeable, and they blend in perfectly. Other details intentionally draw attention to themselves as they perform their task. Best of all, in design there is no single right answer. There are literally millions of solutions to every challenge. All you have to do is let go into the process and allow the creative juices to roll.

My hope is that all the creative details in this book will inspire you to turn your home into your own creative playground. A house that's simply lived in can provide shelter, but it doesn't do much in the way

of inspiration. A house filled with the kinds of details you'll see here can be a highly personal expression of all that has meaning to you. It will be, in a very real way, a reflection of who you really are. And there will be no doubt in anyone's mind that this is HOME in the best sense of the word.

(Left) While performing the role of safety railings, the tapered wood fins and perforated steel planters add depth, texture, and personality.

(Facing page) A large window, oriented to the view, gains visual power through contrast with a small window that offers a mere glimpse.

A single gentle curve impacts the dynamics of a whole space.

<< The smallest trim piece contributes to the overall effect.

Furnishings can be an opportunity to add flashes of color.

> Wide openings allow adjacent rooms to appear larger because they visually borrow space from one another.

Curves and Color Bring a Tiny House to Life

When David and Sukie bought a 1,280-sq.-ft. fixer-upper in Brookline, Massachusetts, back in 1988, they assumed it was a starter home. But Sukie, an avid gardener, fell in love with the soaring paper birch in the backyard, and David, an architect, recognized that the house had great natural light and kept imagining possibilities. Today, their children have gone off to college, but the family remains happily at home in what is still a small house. Remodeling in phases, they updated, opened up the downstairs, and added a garden study with master bedroom above. What makes this modest house so special is the way David and Sukie handled color, light, and scale to unify the house; used curves and small details to add interest; and framed interior views to create a sense of spaciousness.

It might have been tempting to tear down the walls between rooms completely, but David and Sukie had a different idea, one more in keeping with the traditional spirit of the 1920s-era house. They opted to keep the rooms small but to expand the openings between them to 5 ft. or 6 ft.,

outside the house

A Clever Trick for Round Corner Trim

The living room fireplace is a zero-clearance insert; it's housed in a drywall hearth that could be added to nearly any house. Its simple embellishments include a raised granite hearthstone, a gently curved mantel, and round trim made from ordinary wood closet rods, notched to fit the hearth corner as shown in the drawing below. The same closet rod detail is used on the outside corners of the wainscoting.

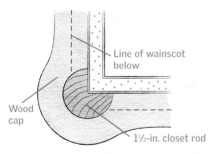

Line of wainscot below

Wood cap

1½-in. closet rod

Living room   The focus of the living room is a hearth that's been added into the space, much as the writing alcove was added to the reading nook (see the left photo on p. 24). Pushing the hearth into the room brings the fireplace closer to the sitting area in the center of the room and creates a pocket of space at either side, perfect for a small table or chair. It's counterintuitive to take away floor space in a small room, but sometimes doing so increases both the distinctiveness and the usefulness of the space.

roughly twice the width of a typical doorway. With four walls intact, each room retains a sense of itself, but the wide openings allow adjacent rooms to appear larger because they visually borrow space from one another.

Take the kitchen and dining room, for example. Sukie and David kept the kitchen as an efficient galley and left the dining room the size it was: big enough for a dining table but no bigger. But where the two rooms used to connect through a doorway, there is now a cooking peninsula under a double arch (see the photo on p. 18). The archway defines a transition area below it and frames the view in either direction. The thickness of the arch also creates a sense of spatial depth. Standing in the kitchen looking through the double arches, you experience the dining room as a place beyond.

A Rectangular Bay Window

A bay window doesn't have to be three windows at an angle to one another. The bay window at the far end of the dining room is a 1-ft. bump-out with a pair of double-hung windows but solid sides that feel like the sides of a really thick wall. The integrity of the bay is enhanced by painting everything within it—window, trim, and walls—the same color. The extra inches expand the space of the dining room and provides enough depth for a narrow window seat, widened here with the barest of curves. It's actually a two-story bay; upstairs, it provides space for bookshelves in a child's bedroom.

 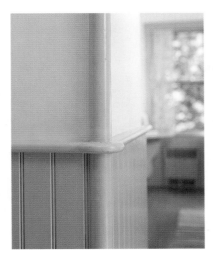 

Harmony through repetition of color and form The pale green color used for all painted wood trim and surfaces throughout the house helps tie together otherwise disparate elements. Less immediately obvious are the lines that embellish the woodwork: for instance, the gouged lines known as "flutes" on the door jambs (see the photo above right) and the newel post (above left), or the grooves—or "beads"—in the bead-board wainscoting. Even the ribbed glass fronts of the kitchen cabinets pick up on the lines.

Simple details add up The cooking peninsula is one of the most attention-getting elements in the house, and yet it's a surprisingly simple construction. The countertop is plastic laminate, softened and spruced up on its edges with wood trim. A similar trim approach has been taken with the tile on the backsplash. The real impact comes from the brackets holding up the counter and forming sides for a display shelf. Each bracket is simply a 1-in.-thick piece of plywood, but the power is in how thoughtfully the plywood has been shaped, and in the concentrated repetition of the curves.

Reading nook   The alcove in the reading nook was created by adding bookshelves within a room just big enough for an overstuffed chair and ottoman. The impression is of a desk set into the extra space within a thick wall, giving the illusion of more space even though there is less floor area than before.

Garden room   A painted wood floor, wainscoting, and ample light from two pairs of windows contribute to the airy, back-porch feel of the garden room. The curved desktop and wavy bracket add some whimsy, while subtle touches like the wide frame around the bead board on the ceiling keep the look crisp.

THE IMPORTANCE OF A CURVE The double arches between the dining room and kitchen add visual interest and frame an interior view. They also define a narrow space in between, an effect enhanced by the bead-board ceiling. If you take away the arches and the bead board, the two rooms bleed into each other, and the transitional space is lost. Remove the curved brackets from the cooking peninsula, and the impact of their refrain is lost as well.

Entry Even a small room like this entry is an opportunity to work with the colors, materials, and details established in the main spaces. The painted floor and ceiling make this a less formal indoor-outdoor space, akin to the garden room, but here the wainscoting is higher, allowing the top trim band to function as a coat rail.

Framed openings aren't the only detail that bring the rooms together. Sukie and David chose a serene palette of colors—cream, sage green, pale spring green, and soft brown—that they maintained from room to room, helping to harmonize the whole house. They also introduced graceful curves throughout the house to break up the somewhat boxy lines of the little rooms. The curves occur at many levels of scale. They can be generous, like the double arches between the kitchen and dining room; whimsical, like the squiggled brackets supporting the garden-room desk or the cooking peninsula countertop; subtle, like the slight sweep of the window seat in the dining room, the fireplace mantel, or the slim writing desk in the reading nook; or unassuming, like the corner trim on the hearth, the molding capping the wainscoting, or the gently rounded trim surrounding the tiled backsplash.

Whether choosing colors, selecting materials, or shaping trim and other details, David and Sukie have been mindful to work with, not against, the diminutive scale of their house. Even the furnishings are in keeping with the scale of house. Most of the furniture pieces are low, making the ceilings feel higher, and the chairs and sofas have legs so that space flows under them. Some might consider this degree of attention fussy, but it's precisely David and Sukie's unwavering approach to detail that makes their tiny house so enduringly livable.

A small, framed interior view hints at space beyond without giving it all away.

Think of a freestanding cabinet as a pod of space, both object and container.

In a simple composition of basic materials, beauty lies in honesty of expression.

A modest house can be beautiful in its simplicity.

Serenity on a Budget

A Not So Big House is not necessarily an inexpensive house. But if you keep the size of the house small and stick with common materials, basic construction methods, and simple details, you can indeed build or remodel on a very limited budget. It helps to pare down your notion of home to its essence and to embrace simplicity—in your house and in your life. But you will not have to give up beauty and delight, nor do without a few special features and spaces that will satisfy your soul.

The retirement house Philip and Nancy built in a passive-solar cohousing community in Durham, North Carolina, offers proof that you can create a tranquil home on a budget that won't raise your blood pressure. When the couple approached architect Tina Govan about designing a simple home, they had read *The Not So Big House* and wanted to incorporate many Not So Big ideas into their home. Tina was equally familiar with Not So Big principles, and she shared the couple's vision of building modestly and efficiently. There was another connection: Tina had worked in Japan; Philip and

outside the house

Hanging shelves, wall shelves Open shelves are not only efficient and inexpensive but also an elegant expression of the very nature of simplicity. Nothing is present except what is absolutely necessary.

picture this

THE IMPACT OF A FREESTANDING OBJECT Although the cabinet is a divider between the dining area and the entry, space slips past it on both sides, maintaining an open feel. Glass display shelves lit from a recessed ceiling fixture add richness; the shelves connect the cabinet to the wall while allowing the cabinet to be seen as an object in space. If the solid cabinet continued to the wall, it would seem more like a peninsula than an island, the flow of space would be interrupted, and the visual energy of the glass shelves would be lost.

Nancy had lived there for a time; and Japanese architectural elements and principles run through *The Not So Big House*. So it was no stretch for Tina to give the house a Japanese leaning, as Philip and Nancy requested.

The house Tina designed, with lots of collaboration from Philip and Nancy, was built within a slim budget yet it provides Philip and Nancy with everything they wanted. Although the house is deliberately spare, the life lived in it is not spartan. Nancy and Philip each have a private space for creative endeavors, and the small second floor is a quiet (and very Japanese) away room with tatami mats for yoga and meditation.

The palette of interior materials is truly minimal: concrete

(sealed but left its natural color) for the main-level floor; drywall (painted white) for all walls, ceilings, and soffits; clear-stained Southern yellow pine for shelving, stairs, and all trim; natural birch plywood for built-ins; standard hollow-core doors; laminate countertops; and basic white appliances. Add shoji screens and tatami mats for the away room upstairs, and that's about it.

An Expressive Hanging Shelf

Even in a minimalist interior, it's possible to create variations on a theme. This wall shelf in the bathroom is simple and inexpensive to build; it's just pine boards and a few lag bolts and screws. It's also visually in tune with similar shelves in the kitchen and, more subtly, with the pattern of thin wood slats on the shoji screen in the living room.

In the kitchen The kitchen isn't a room with four walls but an area separated from the living area by a dropped soffit and a partial wall, and from the dining area by a work island. It could not be more simply appointed: concrete floor, narrow pine storage shelves, and laminate countertops edged with a thin strip of pine.

Dining room The dining area is defined on three sides by a dropped soffit. The soffit is narrow above the doors to the terrace (left) and to the screened porch (right) and wide where it defines the entry area and separates the dining area from the living area. The built-in cabinet provides a further separation between the dining area and the entry area.

detail in focus

A Grid of Under-Stair Storage

The shelves beneath the stairs make the most of what is often unused space. By lining up with the grid of square rails and spindles, the shelves help accentuate the essential stepped nature of the staircase. The staggered ends of the horizontal rails further the stair-step effect. The rails and spindles continue to become the face frames of the shelves. (Even a simple detail like this requires a thoughtful eye for design.)

The way these materials are used, however, is maximal rather than minimal, because the result is the maximum amount of usable space for the least amount of money. Swinging doors and cabinet doors are eliminated wherever possible in favor of pocket doors and open cabinets. Thickened walls contain shelves. Space under the stairs is used for clothing storage on one side and media storage on the other. Aligning the pocket doors eliminates the need for hallways, and the open floor plan reduces the number of interior walls. In several places, the walls between adjacent areas are partial walls; elsewhere, freestanding cabinetry doubles as a wall between two spaces. There are a few items that add cost, namely the shoji screens and the dropped soffit that helps define discrete spaces in the absence of interior walls. But overall, the basic materials and space-saving tactics keep costs well within the limited budget.

Laundry hall The short hall from the kitchen to the bath saves space by doubling as a laundry area. The bath occupies two rooms, one with a sink and commode, the other—seen here beyond the pocket door—with a sink and shower.

The spaces within this unassuming house invariably add up to more than the sum of their off-the-shelf parts. The entry area— just 4 ft. by about 6 ft. 4 in.—is a wonderful example of a space that is small and inexpensive but also hardworking and beautiful. This little entry has a seat with some shoe storage below it, a coat closet, storage cabinets, and two elegant spots for displaying flowers and favorite objects: illuminated glass shelves and a deep, recessed shelf, called a *tokonoma* in Japan. All this, but no expensive materials and no labor-intensive details. The cabinet door pulls are blocks of pine with a curve cut out of them for your hand. Like the rest of the house—the materials, the details, and the spaces themselves—the door pulls are beautiful in their simplicity.

A flexible boundary As the Japanese have known for centuries, a shoji (like other translucent screens) is perfect for creating a flexible degree of openness. Because light passes through it, a shoji screen suggests the space on the other side even when it's closed. This shoji slips neatly into the middle of a two-sided bookcase. Though it's attached to one wall, the bookcase feels like a free-standing object because there's space between it and the ceiling.

Long views and cross-ventilation When the shoji screen is open, the bookcase frames a view from the home office through the living room to the window in the entry area. The entry window lines up with one in the office to generate cross-ventilation as well as long views. The wood tracks on which the shoji slides remain in place to reinforce the framed view.

Minimalist trim for a partial wall The half-walls in the living room are surfaced in drywall with finished corners. A 1x4 strip of wood is screwed to the narrow piece of drywall on the top of the wall, and a 5½-in.-wide strip of finished wood is attached to the wood strip, creating a slight reveal. The effect is richer than the simplicity of the materials and construction would suggest.

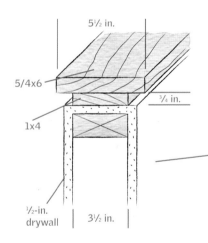

5½ in.

5/4x6

¾ in.

1x4

½-in. drywall

3½ in.

An entry pod The freestanding entry cabinet is a pure expression of a "pod of space," an element that is both an object *in* space and a container *of* space. This pod is both a solid and a void, with storage space concealed behind doors and an open display shelf that in a Japanese house would be called a *tokonoma*. You could place a similar pod beyond a door that opens directly into a living room and, with this move alone, create a defined entry area and add storage.

Simplicity is a state of mind as much as an absence of unnecessary detail.

It's okay to mix >> several kinds of wood in one space as long as they go together.

^^
Positioned just right, even a tiny alcove can take in the whole outdoors.

Although the house has nearly doubled in size, the spaces are still small.

Reinventing the Family Home

Of all types of buildings—museums, libraries, schools, and so on—none is reinvented as often as the house. There's a unique idea of home for every person, couple, family, or group, and for each there's a house to suit. If you and your household can't find what you're looking for in a house that's already built, and if you aren't in a position to build new, you can always find an existing house and reinvent it.

Sabrina and Douglas and their young children have the good fortune to live in Los Angeles, where people and houses reinvent themselves all the time. Douglas, an architect, was able to take a quiet, single-story 1920s Spanish-style house and transform it into a dynamic and contemporary two-story house that fits his growing family as well as the innovative, forward-thinking spirit of the city.

Douglas has a refreshingly open attitude toward how spaces can function in a house. Realizing that the small existing living room would always feel partly like a foyer and acknowledging that his informal family didn't want a

outside the house

A slice of indoor-outdoor space A floor-to-ceiling framed panel of glass cuts diagonally from the end of the family room back toward the kitchen, stealing just enough indoor space from the outdoor terrace for a child's play table. By angling inward, the glass panel avoids blocking the existing windows over the kitchen sink (visible to the left beyond the glass). It also creates a fun triangular space that feels like an adjunct alcove beside the home office alcove (see the floor plan on p. 41).

ACCENT COLUMNS AS ART OBJECTS The antique Thai columns between the dining room and the gallery/foyer are art objects in their own right that add visual weight to the unframed opening and complement the artwork in the gallery. They're also framing devices that contain the view through the opening. Take away the columns and, especially in the absence of trim, the separation between the dining room and gallery/foyer is greatly weakened.

Enter into art Turning the original living room into an open gallery creates a serene welcome space as well as a place for art. A subtle visual trick has been employed on the far wall of the gallery, which has been painted the same color as the others, but three shades darker. This slightly darker wall appears to recede, making the room feel larger.

traditional living room, anyway, Douglas fashioned the living room into an open gallery/foyer for displaying his painting and sculpture and the work of other artists. The family has fewer choices of where to sit, but the open gallery welcomes guests with artwork and provides breathing space for the adjacent dining room and even for the kitchen beyond. Douglas took the same approach with the detached garage in the backyard, which he turned into a full-sized playhouse for his three boys. The garage-turned-playhouse is in full view of the kitchen and just a hop, skip, and jump from the family room. The family room, in turn, occupies space at the back of the house that had been a bedroom and one of two first-floor baths, rendered unnecessary by the second-floor addition.

Upstairs, Douglas's playful approach continues in the

tall, angled spaces. In the master bedroom (see the photo on p. 38), the vaulted ceiling allows for a large 5-ft. by 5-ft. skylight over the bed; in one of the two children's bedrooms, the tall ceiling space is open now but will one day accommodate a sleeping loft, enabling the entire floor to be used for deskwork and play. There's already a ladder concealed in a hall closet that climbs to a secret hideaway above the other children's bedroom.

Translucent wall panel There's more than one way to separate two adjacent spaces. In a traditional house, a half-wall with columns might be one option. In this contemporary house, a translucent glass panel screens the powder-room door but allows light to filter through.

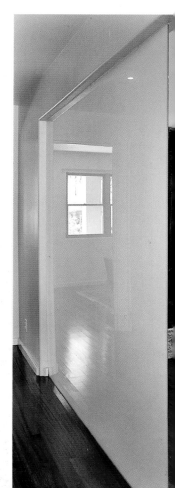

Built-in window seat Here's a great example of a window seat that's been created by building into a room rather than by bumping out, though the effect is similar to a cantilevered bay window. The angularity of the room is softened by the gentle curve in the seat.

A Simple Vanity Mirror

The master bath deftly mixes three sizes of square tiles and three types of green slate, including Kirkstone for the vanity top and the elegant little shelf above the backsplash. The vanity mirror, designed and built by the architect, achieves maximum bang for the buck. It's a simple framed mirror hung on blocking so it floats 1 in. away from the wall. Before it was installed, a standard light track was mounted on the back, facing up, and gooseneck lights were snapped in.

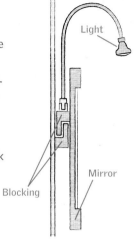

Light

Blocking

Mirror

A number of large and small details contribute to the open and expansive character of the refashioned family room (see the photos on pp. 40–41). Typical of the honest approach this house takes, there's been no attempt to hide the TV. In fact, it's the focal point of a full wall of cabinets. The maple cabinets allow for the depth of the TV at the center, but then they angle back toward the corners of the room. The light-hued maple, the smoothness of the flat-panel doors, and the receding lines keep the cabinetry from overpowering the space. Like the cabinets, the large sliding doors between the family room and the backyard have minimal visual weight.

Clean lines continue in the kitchen, which opens to the family room and dining room. An angled wall of glass creates space for a kid-size play table in the family room without blocking the windows above the kitchen sink. The kitchen proper is no bigger than a stand-up galley, but the countertop steps up to become an eat-in bar for four stools that occupy a narrow space between the dining room and family room. Having the kitchen open to nearly the entire first floor makes it command central for family life. For all its contemporary flair, the house has at its heart the most ancient of communal spaces: a single common area for cooking and eating and living together.

Stairway windows A vertical stack of translucent windows adds light to the stairway while providing privacy at the side of the house.

Concealing a door frame

A sliding door unit includes the doors themselves as well as a larger frame that houses tracks on which the doors slide. Typically, the side pieces of the unit frame abut the sides of the opening, so when the door is closed, you see both door frame and unit frame. But here the fir columns to either side of the door units have a channel cut into them so that the 1-in. unit frame fits within the column. Now when the doors are closed, you see only one frame, not both. It's a subtle bit of streamlining, but it makes a difference.

Calm port in a storm

The home office alcove centered on the wall between the family room and the backyard enables parents to contemplate the garden and keep an eye on the children's playhouse in the converted garage out back. The large window helps the alcove feel like part of the garden and maintains the open feel of the long family-room wall.

Everything in its place

A wall of cabinetry makes the most of the relatively small family room. The TV is in line with the room, as it must be for viewing from the sitting area, but the cabinets and shelves angle back toward the corners of the room. This carefully balanced composition of solid and void, centered on the TV and the floor-to-ceiling stack of cabinets to its right, is far more interesting than uniform cabinets all set to the depth of the TV.

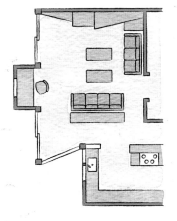

Kitchen-family room connection.

Although the kitchen itself is quite small, it interlocks spatially with the family room. The two rooms, in effect, borrow space from one another. But this kitchen-family room combo is not one large, undifferentiated great room. The low walls and alcoves define distinct areas for sitting, deskwork, play, and cooking, allowing for both expansiveness and intimacy.

Subtle shifts in color make a difference, especially in a simple house.

You don't need expensive materials to make a space more interesting.

When there >> are very few details, each one gains in importance.

The constant play of light is almost the only detail you need.

Classic Cottage Simplicity

This small cottage on Block Island, off the coast of Rhode Island, is the epitome of simplicity. The homeowners came to architect James Estes with a collection of photos of Block Island houses that exhibited traditional cottage elements: weathered gray shingles, porches with low-pitched roofs, and steeply pitched dormers that extend from the face of the house, known, fittingly, as Block Island dormers. What attracted the owners to Block Island was the crisp light and rugged landscape, right out of an Andrew Wyeth painting, as well as the pared-down, no-frills aesthetic of the island's early buildings. They wanted a bare-bones place for themselves and for visits from their grown children and guests.

James designed a house true to classic Block Island cottage form, but he threw in a twist. The roof of the attached front porch continues through the house—where it is the vaulted ceiling of the living room—and comes out the other side as the roof of the back-entry porch. The main

outside the house

Big kitchen window This large double-hung window is a good illustration of leaving well enough alone. Because it is simply trimmed and painted, and because there is nothing around it to distract you, it has a greatly heightened presence, as does the view beyond.

mass of the house has, in effect, been cut in two, and so has two sets of stairs, each leading to dormer bedrooms on one side or the other.

Inside, the bright, open spaces reflect the simplicity and purity of the exterior forms. There's a subtle order, a quietness to the details, and an overarching restraint that is Shaker-like, though the interior is not in the Shaker style. The interior is not without details, of course, but, to a considerable degree, the stripped-down spaces serve as a stage for the ocean, which is the real focus, as it should be at the seaside.

Perhaps the easiest way to understand how the simplicity of the exterior impacts the quality of the interior is to look at the double-hung windows. These windows are really big; on the first floor, they're 3 ft. 10 in. by 6 ft. 9 in., the maximum stock size available from the manufacturer. By scaling the windows larger than our eye imagines they might be, James has made the house appear smaller than it actually is, as well as simpler, more pure in form. Each window sash is divided vertically by just a single muntin, so each window unit becomes a block of four tall panes. These are windows a

Living room The 8-ft.-tall doors and 2-ft.-tall transom windows lend a graceful proportion to the whole living room; you enjoy the spaciousness and the big view but don't feel overwhelmed by the room's height. A crisp order is established when the sliding doors are closed and the vertical door sashes line up precisely with the sashes on the transom windows.

It Takes a Good Plumber

For this cottage, the impact of the large double-hung windows on the exterior was paramount; a smaller window set over the sink would have broken the spell cast by the tall windows and called attention to itself: "Oh, that must be where the sink is!" Leaving the window tall has a playful, stunning impact inside. The sink appears to float, and a plane of light reaches the floor where you'd least expect it. Notice how the window trim, rather than carrying below the countertop, instead turns and becomes the backsplash and then the base trim of the cabinets.

Screened porch The screened porch is a platonic square, stripped of all but its most essential structural elements. Its screen panels, divided by a slim rail, have a graphic visual impact similar to that of the double-hung windows. The strict order of the screen walls, the lack of embellishment, and the pure floor shape make the porch a quiet point from which to sit and watch the ocean.

Bedroom The window perfectly centered on this bedroom dormer reflects the perfection of form seen on the exterior of the house. If the window were off center even a touch, your eye would notice it; you'd feel vaguely unsettled. The simple bed, almost a caricature of itself, further emphasizes purity of form; its vibrant color suits a room this plain.

child would draw. On its sweeping hillside, the simple house shape with its simple windows produces an arresting, agreeable effect.

Inside, the effect is much the same. On the ocean side of the kitchen, a single, oversized double-hung window rests on the baseboard and tops out just shy of the ceiling (see the photo on p. 44). The window's crisp white trim and four oversized panes frame the ocean in a strikingly straightforward manner. Surrounding the window is an unadorned pale gray wall. The ocean captured in the window provides the only true color. The effect is calming, even sublime. Imagine how different the quality of the space (and the view) would be if the wall was paneled in mahogany and the window was divided into 12 panes over 12; you'd perhaps feel you were in a Georgian manor, a very different place from a Block Island cottage.

The living room is, in essence, somewhere between an indoor room and an outdoor room, and the way it is detailed follows suit (see the photo on p. 48). Instead of the smooth drywall ceiling found in the other interior spaces, it has exposed rafters with a tongue-and-groove wood ceiling, all

KITCHEN CABINET NICHE Sometimes, the absence of something is more powerful than its presence. That's the case with the in-fill cabinets between the upper cabinets and the countertop in the kitchen. A display niche has been created by leaving one cabinet unit out; the missing cabinet also allows for more counter space beside the sink. Add a cabinet, and the breathing room and striking niche disappear.

Bath vanity The unexpected but welcome shelf above the master bathroom vanity is a simple, elegant, and highly useful detail, the result of creative design rather than of money spent.

painted white. This ceiling is literally a continuation of the porch ceilings on either side. Although an interior ceiling of exposed rafters looks simple, it raises a challenging question: where to put the insulation? The answer, in this case, is a sheet of rigid foam insulation topped with a sheet of plywood; the two-layer panel is known as a "nail-base" insulation panel because the roofing material can be nailed right onto the plywood layer. The panels are about 4 in. thick, and they sit right on top of the tongue-and-groove ceiling.

Not surprisingly, the living room has the qualities of a porch. Exposed rafters are only part of the reason why. The side walls of the living room are also the sides of the two house pieces split apart by the room; these side walls have been treated as smooth plaster planes to emphasize the form of the house pieces they're part of. In keeping with the sense of the living room as negative space, the entire wall facing the ocean consists of doors and transom windows. In a modern house, such a wall might literally have been all glass, perhaps without any visible frames. Here the doors and transom windows are framed, but the intent is the same: to make this wall disappear so space flows continuously between the living room and the porch, and light pours in.

The right height for a porch rail Porch rails (as well as porch windowsills) are typically set 36 in. above the floor or higher, for safety or to meet code requirements. Unfortunately, high porch rails block the view when you're sitting and greatly diminish the open feeling that draws people out to porches in the first place. The horizontal rails dividing these screen panels are set 30 in. above the floor, about even with the surface of the tabletop.

Defining a dining area It doesn't take a lot to define discrete areas within an open plan. The dining area is divided from the living room by a simply detailed built-in bookshelf and two columns. The second-story wall above the columns is a little lower than the dining-area ceiling, so from within it reads like a beam, further distinguishing the more intimate dining area from the tall living room.

More than meets the eye The twin stairs could hardly be more straightforward, yet each is refined by a surprising number of subtle details. The most obvious refinement is the gracefully tapered newel post. Less immediately obvious are the bottom tread that wraps around the stair wall; the bead-board wall itself, painted a pale gray to emphasize the brighter alternating pattern of white risers and wood treads; the riser and tread pattern; and the railing, which is wood, in contrast to the white spindles.

A thoughtfully controlled color palette creates unity without sameness.

<< The way surfaces capture light affects the entire feel of a room.

Variety in texture >> goes hand in hand with richness of character.

This in-town remodel achieves coherence through imaginative variations on a theme.

A Jewel Box of Texture and Detail

The empty-nester couple who own this house could have bought or built a large house in the suburbs beyond West Hartford, Connecticut, but they chose instead to buy a small house in an older neighborhood, within walking distance of shops, restaurants, and a farmer's market. The couple initially hired architect Jamie Wolf to reconsider the living room, because they didn't like the traditional fireplace or the colonial cabinetry. What began as a consultation about color became a larger conversation about design, then a living-room remodel, and ultimately a transformation of the entire house. Jamie designed an "indoor back porch" that mitigates the elevation change between the kitchen and the cozy backyard; otherwise, the rooms stayed where they were. But the owners encouraged Jamie, and interior designer Peter Robbins, to think boldly (but respectfully) about the opportunities each space presented. The resulting remodel exemplifies richness of detail, imaginative use of space, thoughtfulness in design at every scale, and a balanced use of materials, all executed with an extraordinary degree of craft.

outside the house

Variations on a theme The transformation of the entire house interior began with a remodel of the living room. Ideas, colors, materials, and details established in this room are maintained or reinterpreted in every other room of the house, creating a harmonious whole. Here are just a few examples.

Steel bolts and wire mesh In the living room, black bolts with washers attach the steel mantel to the chimney face. The bolts and washers reappear, polished this time, to attach the railing brackets between the kitchen and the indoor back porch. Wire mesh door panels conceal the existing radiators in the living room; between the kitchen and indoor back porch, wire mesh is fashioned into planter boxes that serve in place of railings.

Details that lean In the living room, the lower cabinets angle, or slant, from the wide speaker cabinets in the corners to the narrow chimney face. This notion inspired tilted or leaning window trim, which energizes a number of windows, such as this one over the kitchen sink.

Groups of squares In the living room, the lower cabinets are divided into squares. In the indoor back porch, a group of three square awning windows is introduced. And in the upstairs study shown at left, the three square windows reappear in slightly different form; the bookcase is a grid that's four squares by four squares, trimmed similarly to the living-room cabinets.

Sunroom The sunroom is detailed to take advantage of its diminutive scale. A room this tiny doesn't handle furniture very well; prop yourself on a chair, and you'd feel like you were on display for passersby. So instead, a futon has been set on a plinth below a wide windowsill. Glass plant shelves span the windows, bringing the room down to the futon level.

Bedroom Wall as Theater

It's amazing how much is happening on this side wall of the master bedroom. Instead of a ho-hum flat wall and a standard door to the dressing room, there's a layered wall with a shoji-like translucent screen that slides on wood tracks to hide behind fabric panels, which seem to float a few inches from the smooth drywall. A soffit above the layered wall brings down the scale of the room (whose high ceiling soars into

what had been attic space) and provides a place for recessed lights. Although this setup is somewhat complex and requires considerable craftsmanship to construct, it is plainly detailed and quite restful, especially at night, when the fabric panels are backlit.

Back hall Often the tall space above a door seems ponderous, but here the deep color of the beige wall and the sculptural light fixture shift the proportions of the entry area, and the door seems just right for the space.

Kitchen planters The planters between the kitchen and the indoor back porch do triple duty, adding texture, serving as a visual screen, and acting as a railing. Notice that one window is divided by muntins and one isn't. People often worry about matching windows precisely, but it simply isn't necessary.

The house isn't lavish—it has no golden chandeliers or marble staircases—but the remodel was not inexpensive. The owners were willing to invest in quality materials and expert craftsmanship as well as in design time for the many things designed expressly for the house. They also invested their own time to collaborate with Wolf and Robbins. What they have for their investment is a home that's tailored to their needs and tuned precisely to their sense of style and expression. At just over 2,000 sq. ft., the house is a finely wrought jewel box, which makes perfect sense when you learn that one of the owners is a jewelry artist.

In redefining the character of the living room

and the tiny sunroom adjacent to it, Jamie arrived at a palette of colors and materials and an approach to details that includes anigre (a light, warmly colored wood) cabinets, pale limestone countertops, wire-mesh door panels, bold but simple steel elements, and glass shelving. These choices were

Kitchen The kitchen features a harmonious mix of materials, textures, and colors. The cabinets are made from two different varieties of wood, not just one. The upper cabinet door panels are a combination of wire mesh and textured glass. Part of the peninsula is stained; part of it is painted. The mix is far more interesting than a whole kitchen of uniform cabinetry bought by the linear foot.

Powder room Small and simple, a powder room is a perfect place to pull out all the stops. In this tiny, playful room, nearly every design idea in the house is given fresh, even whimsical expression. The idea of three square windows, for instance, reappears as three square display niches.

Master bath If the house is a jewel box, the master bath is a gem. The deeper-than-usual tub works for a bath or a shower and is flooded with light cascading from a skylight. The impact of the light is amplified by the contrast between the larger, brighter tiles above the tub and the smaller, darker tiles in the rest of the room.

influenced by practical requirements, of course, but also by Jamie's artistic sense of what feels right. The skewed angle of the low cabinets on either side of the hearth (see the photo on p. 53) can be explained as making up the difference in depth between the deep speaker cabinet in the corner and the narrow chimney face, but the truth is also that the angled cabinet feels right. Same with the curved track for the spotlights above; it just looks good. True, the curve of the track echoes the gentle arc of the limestone mantel, but the track could just as easily be straight.

Design is an exploration of possibilities. As the remodel

continued from room to room, Jamie arrived at fresh interpretations of the ideas introduced in the living room and sunroom. For instance, the black steel bolts that fasten the mantel brackets above the living-room fireplace reappear in polished form to pin wood railings to the half-wall between the

Indoor back porch

Generous sliding doors to the backyard garden keep the 9-ft.-wide indoor back porch from feeling too narrow. The groupings of three awning windows, the tilted window trim above the sliding doors, and the mesh planters and angled wood brackets work together to animate the space and visually relieve its tallness.

THE SUBTLE REFINEMENT OF A
GRID OF SQUARES The stairs
represent one of the last vestiges
of the original neocolonial house.
But the wallpaper, made up of
squares of slightly varied neutral
hues, ties the stair hall to the new
look of the house, where squares
and neutral tones predominate. As
you come to appreciate when it's
taken away, the wallpaper grid also
adds a quiet energy and a measure
of refinement.

Upstairs hall The theme of squares and grids continues upstairs. The double pocket doors open to the hall, turning the entire upstairs into a master suite. When family or friends stay in the guest room, the double doors close, and the hall becomes public space again.

indoor back porch and the kitchen. Jamie also introduced entirely new ideas. Several details that are repeated upstairs first took shape in the indoor porch addition, including the grouping of three square awning windows. Similar windows appear in the stairwell and in the upstairs study. The wallpaper and floating lattice ceiling in the upstairs hallway feature squares meant to echo the awning windows in spirit.

Another detail that first appeared in the indoor porch is a window with trim that leans into the room. Tilting the side trim inward is a simple thing to do, but it generates a subtle energy. In the indoor porch, the tilted trim also emphasizes the thickness of the wall into which the windows are set. But then the lean of the window trim in the vertical is really a variation of the lean of the living-room cabinets in the horizontal, so the lean is not something that first appeared in the porch after all. When a high degree of care and attention has been given to unifying materials, colors, textures, and details, there's almost no end to the connections you can find. It's through unity of effect—which does not mean sameness—that this house achieves coherence.

Archetypal forms >>
like arches and squares
resonate with us
at a deep level.

One of the surest >>
ways to create unity
is through the
repetition of form.

Especially in a
bright and airy house,
dark floors add
solidity and substance.

Finding peace and tranquility is easy in a light-filled home.

Texas Tuscan

You might think that regional styles, by definition, would not be transportable from one region to another. But when the two regions have a similar climate, no matter how far apart they are, the vernacular architecture of one place can befit the other. So it is with Tuscany and Texas—at least those parts of Texas that are both hot and dry. In the arid, hardscrabble land around Austin, Texas, for instance, the villa architecture that evolved in the Tuscan hills makes perfect sense.

All of this came home to architect Steve Zagorski as he traveled in Tuscany, where he was captivated by the small villas dotting the hillsides, which he saw as "basically boxes, with or without ornament." The opportunity to explore Texas Tuscan architecture (as Steve calls it) came when clients Philip and Anne asked him to design a house in Austin that would be small and real rather than large and fake.

The house Steve designed for Philip and Anne is a nearly perfect square (not counting the garage) of roughly 40 ft. by 40 ft. It has a tiled roof, wood pergolas, a narrow portal

outside the house

Punched opening The thick wall between the dining room and the kitchen provides more separation than connection, allowing each space to express itself as an individual room. Even though it's quite wide, the opening between the rooms feels like it's been punched through the wall. The considerable thickness of the wall helps define the countertop, which occupies a kind of transitional space within the wall.

Under-stair storage These inset cabinets and shelves help to express the sculptural quality of the staircase. The archetypal zigzag of the stairs is amplified by the dark stair treads set against the white plaster.

picture this

WHAT A LITTLE DEPTH WILL DO
The niche in the wall under the
stairs allows even small art objects
to have the impact of a much larger
art piece because your eye takes
in the entire composition: the archetypal form of the arch; the sides
of the niche, bathed in light from
above; and the grouping of three
objects. The niche at the far end
of the stair hall has the same effect.
As you can see, two paintings hung
on flat walls would not have the
impact of the two niches.

between the house and the garage, an arched
loggia above the front door, and walls of creamy
Austin limestone. The interior spaces are, by
intention, tall boxes arranged one beside the
other; even the stairwell is a box, albeit two
stories high. This approach to building is not
only true to Texas Tuscan form but also econom-
ical; all else being equal, constructing a series of
boxlike volumes is less expensive than building
complex spaces with lots of ins and outs.

Within the boxy volumes, it's relatively easy
and inexpensive to add a few steps of floor height
or to alter the ceiling, as Steve does in the dining
room with a raised floor and a doubled ceiling
vault known by architects as a "groin vault" (see
the photo on p. 60). The groin vault transforms the walls as well as the
ceiling, giving them an arched shape that mimics the windows and doors.

Above all, it's the shape of the rooms, the thickness of the walls, and the
pure form of the arched openings that connect this house with the villas
Steve saw in Tuscany. The connection is especially powerful because classical
Tuscan architecture relies on archetypal forms that require no translation.
We respond at a deep level to squares and arches, just as we respond
instinctively to the light that's so important in Philip and Anne's house.

The largest and most important space in the house,

the living room, is also the purest expression of Texas Tuscan architecture.
The room is essentially an unadorned 10-ft.-tall space, yet it has tremen-
dous presence (see the photo on pp. 66–67). In many of the houses we've

Up to the den The
steps through the opening
between the living room
and the den are another
feature that emphasizes
wall thickness. Placing the
den three steps above the
living room helps define it
as a distinct space.

Stair central The ethereal character of the interior reaches its apogee in the soaring two-story stair hall. Placing the stairs in the middle of the vertical space gives them a floating, processional quality. The thoughtful placement of religious icons in the twin wall niches lends a contemplative air.

seen, the character of the interior is derived from trim and other distinctive built-in details, from the shapes of the spaces, even from the furnishings. In this living room, all that falls away, leaving the arched openings, the stone chimney and end wall, and the light streaming in. Imagine the same space with Oriental carpets, upholstered chairs, dark wood paneling, and thick trim. It might be a beautiful room, but much of the light would be absorbed by the rich materials. With so much else to consider, we might not focus as readily on the light.

For many of us in this country, our sense of home derives from the northern climates of England, Germany, and Scandinavia. We equate comfort with sitting in a cozy inglenook by the fire, safe from the howling winds. In the temperate zones, a tall stone and plaster box like Philip and Anne's living room probably wouldn't conjure up the feelings of warmth we associate with home. But the situation in a hot, dry place like Austin is very nearly the opposite of what it is in the vast temperate regions of our continent. A tall space where the hottest air stays above us feels welcoming indeed. Just looking at the stone and plaster, we sense the absence of the heat they are absorbing.

The radiant and transporting quality of sunlight may have very definite connotations in an Italian church; in a house, the effect of light is equally profound if less numinous. Quite apart from whatever spiritual beliefs we may hold, we all respond to light and can find great peace and tranquility in a light-filled home.

Second-floor loggia In many center-hall houses, a bath or closet occupies the space above the front door and foyer. Here a small, covered terrace (or *loggia*) offers a quiet, shaded place between the master bedroom and study. The loggia is just 9 ft. 4 in. by 10 ft 4 in., but it makes all the difference.

Forced Perspective

The tub alcove in the master bathroom plays with Renaissance notions of symmetry and perspective. Although the alcove looks grand, it's simply a standard tub built into a 6-ft.-wide alcove between the water closet and shower. The tub is set a little high, allowing for a gracefully curved step. Plain, tumbled limestone tiles are embellished with decorative ceramic tiles (a great way to get maximum impact from just a few expensive tiles). The deep arch over the tub is angled to create a forced perspective, a trick of the eye favored by Italian painters and sculptors. The point isn't to fool anyone but to have some fun and punch up the visual appeal of the bath.

Making a little stone go a long way Stone on an interior wall is expensive because it has to be laid to the inside of a wood-framed, insulated wall; stonework thus takes the place of much less expensive trowel-finished drywall. By featuring stone on the most prominent wall in the house, the whole interior of the main floor benefits. The impact of the stone is heightened by doors to either side of the hearth that let you experience the doubled stone wall by passing through it.

Surfaces as a stage for light What you experience in the living room is not just light itself but the play of light on the reflective surfaces of the thick plaster window openings and the glossy wood floor.

Form and light in combination The archetypal form of the arch figures prominently in the living room and is repeated throughout the interior, as in the dining-room window. The character of this window vignette is derived primarily from the interplay of the thick arched opening and natural light in the absence of distractions from heavy details or furnishings.

Repetition of form The niche at the foot of the stairs mirrors the arched windows in form, and, like the windows, it helps express the thickness of the walls. The recessed light illuminates the small painting, but it also accentuates the sides of the niche, just as sunlight accentuates the sides of the arched window openings.

<< A twist of 45 degrees may be all it takes to make the old appear new again.

<< Size the roof overhangs right, and you won't need curtains to block the sun.

An underlying ordering system lends coherence to every detail in the house.

Logic and order are immediately apparent in this "pinwheel" house.

Order in the Details

Most architects would agree that design constraints—modest budgets, odd-shaped sites, height restrictions—are a virtue because they channel creativity along certain lines. Paradoxically, the challenges imposed by limits can be more compelling than the unfettered freedom of a blank slate. So architect Frederick Noyes had a good thing when a retired couple asked him to design a one-story cottage for their visiting children and grandchildren (and for themselves should they no longer be able to negotiate stairs). The hitch? The cottage could be no bigger than 800 sq. ft., the maximum allowable size for a second house on their property on Martha's Vineyard, Massachusetts.

To make the most of so little space, Fred actually imposed further constraints by establishing two underlying ordering systems. One ordering system is the pinwheel form of the house: a tall main space in the center with four smaller spaces overlapping like spokes around it. The other ordering system is a 6-ft. module that regulates everything

outside the house

Entry The overlap of space between the main living/dining room and the smaller spaces surrounding it is subtle but effective. The wood-paneled wall and the brick floor define the entry area proper, but the floating beam extends the entry experience ever so slightly into the tall volume of the main space. It also defines a transition area between the main space and the lattice porch.

from the arrangement of the interior spaces to the placement of walls and windows to the nature of details.

The two ordering systems unify the house. Even though you may not see the 6-ft. module, you experience it. The interior spaces feel crisp and composed, yet there isn't a quality of stiffness or rigidity about the house. This is because the pinwheel form generates layered volumes that share space in a dynamic way, one borrowing from the next. Space flows easily between the smaller spaces (bedrooms and kitchen) and the main space (living and dining area), and between the main space and the outdoor spaces (lattice porch, screened porch, and open deck).

Natural light also enlivens the spaces. Because the glass gable ends of the tall main space face east and west, they transmit even light across the vaulted white ceiling for most of the day. Stronger, more direct light hits the screened porch, the lattice porch, and the small kitchen window; thus, the brightest light dances around the edges of the main space, animating it without overwhelming (or overheating) it. The drama of natural light combined with the overlapping of space makes the house seem much larger than its square footage.

detail in focus

Built-In Bedroom Utility

The master bedroom with vaulted ceiling is, in essence, a smaller version of the main living/dining space. A horizontal band of fir, not unlike the floating beam in the larger main space, defines a dresser niche and a desk niche on either side of a closet. The horizontal band makes more sense in this open interior than a solid-walled soffit would. People worry needlessly about matching wood; here, the fir trim nicely sets off the birch closet doors and dresser.

Living-room hearth The rectangular panel of the chimney brick and the solid wall panel above the mantel help emphasize the pure geometry of the wood framework. In a similar manner, extending the glass gable windows to the ceiling plane emphasizes the pure form of the vaulted ceiling, which almost seems to float free of the end wall.

An implied soffit A floating beam defines the portion of the main living/dining space shared by the kitchen. The beam functions like an implied soffit above the kitchen island, creating a more intimate sitting area. At the same time, it brings down the apparent height of the living/dining space, keeping it from feeling too tall. And the beams attached laterally to the main beam provide an anchor for light fixtures and open shelves.

Honest shelves The shelving unit is simply an open box (birch plywood faced with strips of solid birch) clipped to the floating beams with steel brackets. Everything is on display, not just the glasses and dishes but the brackets and the shelves themselves. Open shelves provide a degree of separation between the kitchen and the living/dining room while allowing space to flow freely.

The result of order, not expense The appliances, countertops, cabinetry, and wood shelves in this kitchen could hardly be more ordinary. Their crisp, tidy look is not the result of money spent but of time taken to establish a loose symmetry about the window at the center, to line up beams with cabinets, and to work with the 6-ft. module that underlies the organization of the entire house. The clean composition gives simple elements like stock cabinets and a plain wood backsplash a dignity they wouldn't have if they'd been put together haphazardly.

Lattice porch In a house that doesn't draw hard lines between inside and out, the lattice porch feels like a room even though it is clearly an outdoor space. The roomlike nature of this minimally enclosed porch is partly the result of having the same dimensions and volume as the screened porch and each of the bedrooms.

picture this

DEGREES OF ENCLOSURE The west gable end of the main living/dining space is divided into panels by fir framing members. Fixed glass fills each of the panels except the hearth panel, creating a strong connection between inside and outside and enabling the wide roof overhang and the angled brick chimney to be experienced from the main space. The overall effect of the wall would be very different if more of the panels were solid wall.

The way the interior is detailed reinforces both the quality of light and the feeling of overlapping space. In detail after detail, openness is emphasized. Where there could have been a solid wall above the hearth, instead there are smartly framed clerestory windows. Over the kitchen, where you might expect a solid soffit, there is an open frame of floating beams. In place of a kitchen cabinet with doors is an open grid of shelves. What could have been a solid beam spanning the center of the main living/dining space becomes a doubled beam with a slim gap of space between the planks.

The main space is a perfect square in plan, which you might think would make it a static place. But the two free-floating beams that stretch between the gable ends and the double beam that crosses the center of the space divide the square into implied rectangles. The floating beam on the south side of the main space helps define the kitchen area, which occupies a portion of the main space as well as its own

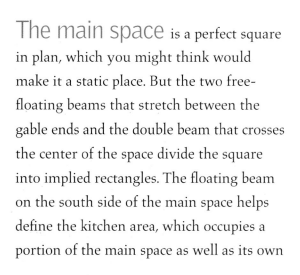

In the corner Glass doors and panels of fixed glass break down the corner of the living/dining room so that space seems to continue into the screened porch. Being able to see into adjacent spaces makes the house feel larger than it actually is.

Two-door bathroom
Bathrooms with two doors can make guests uncomfortable, but in this tiny house, where everything has to do double duty, two doors enable the bath to serve both the children's bedroom and the entry area, which shares a hardworking brick floor with the bath.

Double-duty bathroom A pleated window shade is cleverly used to conceal the stacked washer/dryer from the rest of the master bath. A closet door would have gotten in the way of the door to the room.

smaller space. Likewise, the floating beam on the north side of the main space creates a subtle transition zone just beyond the tiny entry area. These beams are set exactly 3 ft. (half of a 6-ft. module) into the main space, and because everything conforms to the same modular system, the beams line up precisely in the center of a 6-ft. window-and-door module to either side of the hearth, which, no surprise, is itself 6 ft. wide (see the photo on p. 71).

If you're quick with math, you'll have figured out that the main space is 18 ft. by 18 ft., three modules by three modules. But the point of a modular system is not mathematical rigor; it is clarity of expression, beauty, and beyond that, delight. It is a house whose logic and order are immediately apparent. The materials and details are simple and straightforward. To the degree that they draw attention to themselves, they also accentuate the qualities of light, order, and spaciousness inherent in the overall design. It would be hard to say which you like better in a house as tightly conceived as this, the parts or the whole.

<< A dark, rough-surfaced wall adds visual weight and catches your attention.

<< The differentiation of parts generates contrast, drama, and personality.
v
v

Presented honestly, a material can be beautiful just by being exactly what it is.

In this modern row house, the absence of trim has its own visual strength.

A Spare House that Sparkles

Although it's been more than 100 years since the first stirrings of modernism, modern architecture, particularly as a house style, has yet to become part of the vernacular. In its pure form, modern may never be a style for most people. And yet we can all benefit from exploring a well-designed modern house. In a modern house, the details, materials, and design ideas that make up a successful home interior are presented in a very clean, stripped-down fashion. The lessons a modern interior teaches are right there in front of us, not hidden behind layers of trim and decoration.

For adherents of modern design, this extreme level of honesty, simplicity, and straightforwardness is precisely the appeal. Take the striking row house unit architect Kevin DeFreitas designed for Stewart, a single professional. Stewart's home is part of a 17-unit row house "village" Kevin designed and built in downtown San Diego. The row houses make highly innovative use of tilt-up concrete panels (the precast slabs often used for huge warehouses)

outside the house

Dining room/kitchen connection A wide opening with a transom window above creates a strong connection between the dining room and kitchen. Solid pocket doors (at right) provide privacy when the dining room is used as a guest bedroom, while the transom window still allows light into the kitchen.

detail in focus

A Skillful Trick of the Eye

Good architecture sometimes equals a good illusion. The combination of a large vanity mirror, a wide opening with opaque glass doors, and large windows at the front and back of the house lends this tiny bath a sense of space it doesn't actually possess. The key to this illusion is extending the vanity mirror over the entire wall behind the sink; with a smaller framed mirror, the illusion wouldn't be half as effective.

as multistory walls separating the units. And yet the inspiration to build narrow, densely packed houses came to Kevin on a trip to Baltimore, where he was impressed by the intimate streetscapes of traditional row houses. Kevin's contemporary row houses reflect a love of the modern aesthetic shared by Stewart and the other homeowners, as well as a respect for the time-honored pleasures of a walkable city neighborhood.

A valuable lesson, for modernists and traditionalists alike, lies in the way Kevin has differentiated the various materials and parts of the interior so that each gains in visual importance. In Stewart's row house, everything—architectural elements, furniture, art—stands out individually, which allows us to appreciate its essential form, texture, and color—its

Floating wall The open, floating quality of this wall of kitchen cabinets combined with the open stairway keep the kitchen from feeling too narrow. The space above and below the upper cabinets contributes to the openness, as does the black toekick, which helps the lower cabinets appear to hover above the floor.

Defining wall The need to conceal plumbing pipes and heating ducts gave rise to the thickened white wall built out from the concrete side wall. The white wall defines the kitchen area and bounces light around this potentially dark space. Small, lit niches punched into the white wall playfully accentuate its thickness and reveal the concrete wall behind.

essential nature. The generous openness of the space and the intensity of the light that spills in serve to heighten this effect. Concrete walls, aluminum-framed windows, or an uncarpeted floor may feel cold to some, but the clarity of individual elements is what gives this row house interior its drama and character.

With no trim or ornamentation to distract us, we experience precisely what is special about the natural grain of the maple floor, the roughness of the concrete, the smoothness of the drywall, the stairs as an archetypal form, the pattern of the perforated window screen, the cool, green reflectivity of the glass kitchen backsplash.

At the detail level, the differentiation of parts is most palpable where parts and materials come together. In a traditional home, the meeting of two parts or two materials is generally an occasion for trim to bridge the gap,

A WALL WITH VISUAL WEIGHT
A rough texture and relatively dark color give the concrete side wall added visual weight and thus greater impact on the ambience of the room. The gray wall provides a rich background for the yellow and blue chairs and especially for the red painting; the dark wall is also a foil for the white couch and lamp. If we make the wall smooth and white, it loses its power.

however small that gap may be. As we see in so many outstanding traditional homes throughout this book, trim presents an opportunity for added visual interest and delight, as well as for regulating lines that help us make sense of a space. But a lack of trim can have power, too. In this modern row house, the crisp, clean joints between one part and another have their own kind of visual intensity.

Good modern design can make simple look beautiful and small feel spacious. Thus a modern house can be (though it isn't always) highly affordable. The Swedish manufacturer and retailer IKEA® has exploited the inherent economy of modern design to make elegant yet affordable furniture, and here Kevin DeFreitas has done it in a row house.

In a conventional row house —one with boxy rooms,

framed doorways, narrow hallways, and double-hung windows of modest proportions—light has a hard time finding its way to the middle of the house, and the rooms can feel exceedingly cramped. Stewart's row house is 52 ft. long and just 15 ft. 2 in. wide, but three hallmarks of modernism—floor-to-ceiling walls of glass, an open floor plan, and minimal trim—give the spaces breathing room. In this case, the modernist approach also saves money: The tilt-up concrete walls are at once structure and interior and exterior finish; the glass walls at either end are relatively inexpensive commercial storefront construction with off-the-shelf windows; the kitchen cabinet doors are from IKEA; and the stairs are simply stock lumber from a home center. The elegance and the beauty are in the intrinsic virtues of each material and in how it all comes together.

Wall niche A full wall of cabinets would have provided more storage in the dining room, but the open niche with its deep purple wall gives the whole room a sense of greater depth, serves as a sideboard, and adds a splash of color.

Wall as headboard The black accent wall built out from the concrete side wall serves double duty, concealing plumbing from the kitchen below while serving, in effect, as a giant headboard to define the sleeping area. The sleeping area is further defined by the curve of the wood floor where it meets the slate tile of the sitting area. A drop-down "nightstand" takes advantage of the thickness of the headboard wall.

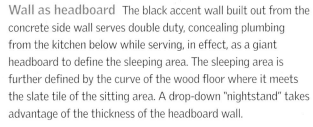

Planelike white walls add drama In true modernist fashion, the two white walls in the bedroom appear as pure planes, seemingly independent of the surrounding structure. The wall with the painting, set against the wood cabinetry and brightly lit from a skylight above, almost vibrates with energy. The parapet wall above the stairs, connected to the concrete sidewall by a clear glass panel, seems to leap forward as it slices down the middle of the space.

Many layers in just a few inches The Mondrian-like pattern of the aluminum window and door frame establishes a thin, transparent layer between the roof deck and bedroom. The black steel frame—required for earthquake safety— adds another subtle layer, as do the motorized, roll-down screen and privacy shades. A great number of visual effects, light conditions, and degrees of privacy are possible, depending on whether the doors are open or closed and on the position of the screen and shades.

There's an elusive
yet undeniable charm
in the simple fairness
of a curve.

A very small house
can achieve the snugness
and refinement of
a tailored suit.

Particleboard is
a perfectly decent
material when it's
treated with integrity.
v
v

Economy reigns in a floating home where every inch counts.

A Houseboat Full of Nautical Charm

A wooden boat is the essence of the maxim "a place for everything and everything in its place." In the necessarily compact cabin of a sailboat, every square inch must be used, and in a well-crafted wooden boat, every square inch is also lovely to look at. All Not So Big Houses embrace a kind of graceful economy, but perhaps none more so than a small floating house, occupying as it does a middle point between a house and a boat.

Having scouted fishing boats for 20 years with vague domestic notions in the back of their minds, recent empty-nesters Barry and Val pared down their possessions, sold their 3,000-sq.-ft. house in Idaho, and moved into a dilapidated 700-sq.-ft. single-story houseboat on Lake Union in Seattle, Washington. They kept the floating log "footprint" of the 1920s houseboat, but little else remains beyond one porthole and the charm of the original, reinterpreted in two stories and an aesthetic that combines 1920s Craftsman-style bungalow and 1960s cabin cruiser. Barry and Val are part of a diminutive floating community of kayaks and ducks and creative

outside the house

Window seat The bright window seat at the top of the stairs is a made-to-order reading spot for a book picked from the stairway bookshelves. The seat lifts up to reveal storage underneath.

neighbors, with sweeping views of the Space Needle and the Seattle skyline crisscrossed by the comings and goings of seaplanes. But it's inside, where the artfulness of boatbuilding meets the art of home building, that this little house comes into its own as a comfortable nest for empty-nesters.

Storage is a theme running through the house. As often as not, a seemingly mundane storage problem gives rise not only to a functional solution but also to an unexpected flourish. For example, what appear to be column bases at either side of the fireplace turn out to be pull-out shelves for videos and CDs (see the top left and bottom right photos on p. 89). Similar pull-out shelves are fitted into even the slimmest sections of the kitchen and entry area. The one TV in the house swivels around in its cabinet to face either the living room or the bedroom. The stairway doubles as a library, with shelves on three sides marching upward with the steps. The

---

the way it's done

Window Seat With Rollaway Bed

This window seat in a cozy corner of the second-floor workspace turns into a bed with a few elegant moves that call to mind the compact economy of a VW™ camper perhaps more than a boat cabin. The drawer (which is a useful storage bin) rolls out to become, along with the seat top, a base for a double bed. A hinged plywood panel folds down to the opened drawer. One of two pads (previously stacked together as a seat cushion) is simply pulled forward over the drawer to complete the bed.

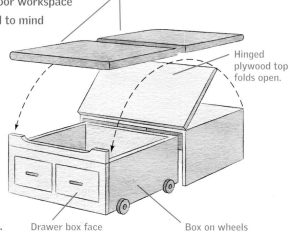

Two pads (stacked for seat)

Hinged plywood top folds open.

Drawer box face

Box on wheels

Library stairs The stairway as library is one of the most pleasing and useful elements you can incorporate into a new house or a remodel. With the addition of just 10 in. on all sides, the stairway becomes a room full of books. You might think books would overwhelm a small space, but their visual richness is, if anything, more enchanting in this tight stairway, with its lighthouse-shaped newel posts and arched ceiling.

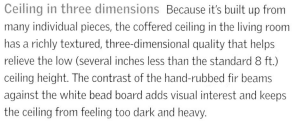

Ceiling in three dimensions Because it's built up from many individual pieces, the coffered ceiling in the living room has a richly textured, three-dimensional quality that helps relieve the low (several inches less than the standard 8 ft.) ceiling height. The contrast of the hand-rubbed fir beams against the white bead board adds visual interest and keeps the ceiling from feeling too dark and heavy.

A nautical echo Subtle thematic connections invariably enhance the character of a house. The round vintage photograph in its circular frame feels just right above the mantel, though it's hard to say exactly why—until you see the ship's porthole around the corner.

Furniture-quality cabinetry and a boatbuilder's approach to storage Fine craftsmanship is especially appropriate in a very small house, where it can't help but be seen from up close; craftsmanship is also more affordable in a small house, where there isn't too much to detail. These cherry cabinets have slim, shiplike proportions and trim lines, with flat panels set off by what's known to furniture makers as a parting bead. The panels under the columns cleverly slide out to reveal storage shelves, just as they might in a boat.

The perfect spot for a TV Half-hiding the television behind leaded-glass doors to one side of the fireplace maintains the classic look of the hearth and its surrounding cabinetry. In a house where everything does double duty, the TV is no exception: It swivels within its cabinet so it can be viewed from the bed in the master bedroom.

Windows to Bathe By

This nearly open-air tub is the bathing equivalent of a corner window seat. The clear glass of the adjacent shower, the glossy white walls and trim, and the tall casement windows contribute to the airy quality of the bath. White curtains hung gingerly from thin metal cables provide privacy without diminishing the open feel; the cables are like the guy lines of a sailboat, in keeping with the nautical character of the house. But it's the way the windows meet the lip of the tub that has the greatest impact on the bathing experience. Bringing windows right down to tub level is really the only way to ensure a view for a bather lying back in a tub.

Kitchen   Among the many smart appointments in this efficient kitchen are two ideas that make sense in a kitchen of any size. One is to continue the countertop material up to the windowsill to create a simple and elegant backsplash, as has been done here with soapstone. The other is to build separate cooktop and oven units into the lower cabinetry, avoiding the awkward, vaguely out-of-place look of some single-unit ranges.

A SCULPTURAL HEARTH The woodwork surrounding the fireplace takes full advantage of the narrow space under the soffit. The wall has substantial presence even though it's just 2 ft. wide at its widest. The stepped appearance of this paneled wall is accentuated by the built-up moldings, the brackets under the mantel, and especially the short columns. The space between the columns and the wall is as critical as the columns themselves to the sculptural quality of the composition, as you can see when the columns are removed.

space under the stairs (accessible from outside) holds bicycles, snowboards, fishing gear, and anything else you might imagine in an attic or garage.

Yet the houseboat never feels cramped, whether

you're upstairs under the bowed ceiling or downstairs in the kitchen, living room, bedroom, and bath. Barry and Val have a modest amount of stuff and lead tidy, disciplined lives, but that only explains the lack of clutter, not the overall feeling of tranquility. The calm character of the interior stems as much from the beauty of its proportions as from the thoughtfulness of its parts.

The living room is a pleasing 16 ft. by 16 ft. square, richly appointed with dark fir wainscoting, beams, and trim. With just a single seating area in front of its substantial hearth and a small dining table off to one side, it feels satisfyingly snug and cozy.

The living room feels calm, not cramped (and this could apply to any space in the house), because Barry has shown admirable restraint. There's a ton of storage tucked into the house, but, strictly speaking, there's room for a ton more. Barry has the good sense to provide enough storage but not so much that shelves and drawers and cabinet doors overwhelm the spaces. There's lots of wood paneling, cabinetry, and trim, but in every case the dark wood is balanced by white space, whether it's painted bead board or swatches of drywall. The spaces themselves are simply not crammed too full of furniture and artwork and other stuff, so even in this tiny cocoon, there's ample room to breathe and grow.

French doors French doors extend the living-room space onto the waterside deck, establishing a beguiling contrast between the tidiness of the paneled interior and the jumbled neighborhood of floating decks, boats, and houses.

Contrasting levels >>
of artificial lighting
are more interesting
than even lighting.

<< One wall painted
a different color can
alter the character
of a whole room.

An underlying order,
like meter in a poem,
gives a space its rhyme
and reason.

A carefully controlled system of artificial lighting defines spaces without dividing them.

Defining Space with Light

We respond naturally and deeply to sunlight and firelight, and almost as intensely to electric lighting, our surrogate candle beam. Most of us pay attention to natural light in our homes, appreciating it when it's abundant, finding ways to bring in more of it (with added windows, skylights, or sunrooms) when it's lacking. Too often, though, we give short shrift to artificial lighting. We make do with what we have—maybe putting a brighter bulb in the ceiling fixture or installing a strip of track lighting. This is a shame, because artificial lighting represents an opportunity to make a huge difference in the character and quality of a home at a very reasonable cost.

Architect Bruce Rogers understands the value of good lighting because in his first career he was a theater set designer. Bruce and his wife, Jane Kuelbs, also an architect, made artificial lighting an integral part of the design when they remodeled their home in Evanston, Illinois. Their 1895 farmhouse had been converted into a two-family flat,

outside the house

Saving dough and rolling it out The amount of cabinetry was kept to a minimum in this streamlined kitchen, making more affordable the custom anigre-faced cabinets designed by homeowner and architect Bruce Rogers. The easy-to-clean stainless countertop is set at a standard 36-in. height for the cooktop; the white marble countertop, ideal for baking projects, is set at 39 in. to make it easier to roll out dough.

A cozy kitchen niche Because of their height and depth, refrigerators and floor-to-ceiling cabinets are hard to place in a small kitchen, especially if the kitchen does not have upper cabinets elsewhere to balance the bulk. Separating the refrigerator and oven cabinet along an exterior wall creates a slim but useful work niche (the homeowner calls it a "coffee altar").

The way house parts come together In this crisp, modern remodel, no trim is used to hide the joint where two materials meet. There's no frame around the inset wall cabinet, for instance; instead, the wood meets the drywall cleanly, separated by a narrow reveal. (A metal edge called a J-bead keeps the edge of the drywall sharp.) Look again at the photo on the facing page, and you'll see a reveal between the oven cabinet and the drywall.

Places defined with light Even though this free-flowing family space is broadly lit, point lighting has been used subtly to mark three distinct areas within it. A paper lantern signals the TV/play room; a beam of spotlight on the green wall signals the dining room; and the marble countertop reflecting light from downlights on the ceiling above signals the kitchen.

its modest 1,000-sq.-ft. first floor chopped into nine small rooms. The couple wanted a more open, flexible place for themselves and their young son and an efficient kitchen where they could both cook at the same time.

The question Bruce and Jane asked themselves

was this: Keeping to a minimalist aesthetic (which is, in fact, part of the answer), how do you define many spaces without dividing the house into tiny rooms all over again? Part of the solution was to turn the load-bearing walls at the front and back of the long, thin house into partitions that define spaces without enclosing them. These partition walls, painted a pale green, are pulled away from the exterior walls, so that light—natural or artificial— slips around them, subtly connecting a reading area with the living room at the front of the house and a TV/play space with the dining room and kitchen at the back. A continuous ceiling plane, uninterrupted by framed doorways, further unites the spaces, making them all appear larger. The spaces are arranged so that light and partial views draw you through them. You glimpse the living room from the entry, the dining room from the living room, the TV/play room from the dining room. Space is ever unfolding.

Back to the question of defining spaces without dividing them, a big part of the solution is a carefully controlled system of artificial lighting. *System* is really too severe a term for the subtle impact of lighting in this house, though all of the lights downstairs are indeed operated by two control panels. The controllers enable Bruce to dim lights individually or in groups, as well as to program a number of preset vignettes, or scenes, with lighting levels set optimally throughout the spaces for dining or entertaining.

Not surprisingly, given his first career, Bruce takes a theatrical approach to lighting. Rather than dumping a lot of bright light into a space, Bruce

A Trick of the Eye

We see light emanating from the pendant and assume it is falling on the dining table. In fact, the pendant throws off very little light; its role is to create a warm focal point. The table is actually lit by four recessed downlights placed roughly above the table corners. Meanwhile, the twin spotlights highlight the photo and bounce a little ambient light from the wall, and sunlight spills through the gap in the wall, adding more ambient light.

prefers to spotlight an important object—often a painting or photograph on the wall—and to allow just a little ambient light to bounce off the object into the space. In a similar vein, he uses lights to delineate specific areas within a room, such as a group of chairs or the dining table, leaving the spaces between the lit areas a little darker. Light thus provides contrast within rooms as well as between them, helping to define discrete spaces subtly but just as surely as might a column, a low wall, a panel screen, or a lowered ceiling soffit.

With lighting there is a paradoxical freedom that comes with control: Simply put, more is possible with a dimmer switch than without. The same could be said about order in architecture. An ordering system can be surprisingly liberating. Bruce and Jane studied the original footprint of the house to establish a regulating grid of 16-in. squares. This

grid of regulating lines then helped them locate everything from kitchen tiles to new walls and windows to light fixtures, all without generating visual confusion. To the contrary, the 16-in. grid helps relate the various house parts to each other, creating a more calm, comfortable, and cohesive whole.

Reading chair The round lamp adds ambience and marks the chair as a special place to sit (while recessed ceiling lights provide light for reading). The vignette of chair, table, wall art, and light presents itself to the entry, announcing that you're in a modern house.

In threes Groups of three give these minimalist stairs a crisp sense of order. The three round step lights line up with three pairs of metal balusters, and the three photos continue the scheme. You may not notice the repetition of threes at first, but you feel the rhythm.

picture this

LIGHT TO WALK TOWARD There's something alluring about light glimpsed in the distance that piques our interest and draws us forward. The illuminated pendant over the table and the spotlit photo (set against the green accent wall) stretch space from the living room into the dining room. Take away the light (and the distinctive wall color), and the effect is lost.

<< A coherent design can bring polished mahogany together with whitewashed pine.

In the effort to >> get everything right, don't forget to have fun.

The one rule of eclecticism is this: If it fits, it fits.

Vintage materials and a playful attitude lend an informal air to this modest beach house.

Laid-Back Florida Cracker

Architects are sometimes criticized for liking their work too much ever to allow curtains or drapes to hide any of it. In this architect's own house, curtains were part of the design from the beginning. Evoking a time gone by, the cottage has no formal closets; in place of closet doors, simple curtains hang from galvanized rods. In a similar vein, operable shutters filter light from the front porch; the baths are outfitted with freestanding porcelain tubs; and the doorknobs are old rimlocks from the late 1800s.

Architect Jim Strickland designed this remarkable beach retreat in WaterColor, Florida, for himself and his wife, Linda, and their extended family. Although it's a new house, it's meant to look and feel like a laid-back fish camp that's been passed down from generation to generation. Authenticity is paramount in the design, along with informality and durability. Harkening back to cottages he remembered as a child, Jim created an inspired meld of simple spaces, vintage materials and fixtures, and well-worn

outside the house

furnishings that manages to feel honest and inviting without ever seeming too precious. In just more than 2,000 sq. ft., Jim has also slipped in a modern heating and cooling system, contemporary appliances, and four bathrooms. The cottage may look and feel like a Florida cracker, as such a house is called in the regional vernacular, but it's as comfortable and convenient as any new home.

Jim's architectural firm, Historical

Concepts, designs new buildings that have the patina of age, so it's no surprise he employed a trick or two in his own cottage for creating a vintage look. His approach is widely applicable, even in a house that doesn't aim for a strict historical effect, because it relies on using inexpensive building materials in imaginative ways and celebrating the imperfections of old fixtures, worn furnishings, and family hand-me-downs, many of which can be had for a song. It might seem easier to be playful and informal in a second home, but there's no good reason not to adopt the same attitude with a primary residence. If you're on a limited budget, then using reclaimed or inexpensive materials will save you money and may allow you to pick and choose a few key materials or elements on which to splurge.

Barn door The barn door between the master bedroom and bath makes sense because there isn't enough room for a door swing. A sliding-panel door feels at home in a house where opened shutters and curtains (like the one at right in the photo) remain visible. A pocket door would work but is less in keeping.

Stair hall and master bath The trim on the wall in the stair hall illustrates the idea of a simple pattern overlay. The grid pattern of the trim breaks up the large wall surface into smaller panels, adding visual interest and creating an order that helps position the family photos. In the master bath, the grid of trim lends order to the photos, the mirrors, the towel hook, and the antique gas lights (rewired for electricity).

Framed opening A framed door opening with transom window above separates the stair hall from the living room in a way that makes the stair hall appear almost as outdoor space, maintaining the easy indoor-outdoor quality that begins on the front porch.

Front porch Operable shutters give the porch a vintage feel, but they're not just for looks. Like operable shutters of old, these provide cooling shade, privacy from a street that's only steps away, and shelter from inclement weather.

Utilitarian kitchen furniture Because the cabinets stop at various distances from the ceiling and they're topped with strong crown moldings, they feel more like old-fashioned kitchen furniture pieces than contemporary built-in cabinetry. In place of rows of matching cabinets, there's a mix of open shelves, small, breadboard-like countertops, and cabinet units with the loose feel of stacked Shaker boxes.

Functional appeal Placing a dish rack across the kitchen window is a brilliant way to provide both light and privacy at the side of the house, where the neighbors are so close you could ask them to pass the salt. A dish rack has the straightforward appeal of utility. Similarly, the contemporary stainless-steel range makes sense in this kitchen because, like the dish rack, its beauty lies in its pure expression of functionality.

No need to match Many contemporary kitchens feel monolithic, the result of too much cabinetry made from a single wood, with floors, walls, and trim of the same or a very similar hue. This kitchen features a variety of wood species and other materials, held together not by literal sameness but by a shared sensibility. Mahogany French doors, whitewashed pine walls, painted wood trim and cabinetry, and stained heart pine countertop: Each, in its fashion, is a simple and honest expression of its purpose.

A Child's Bed with a Pedigree

This child's bed is set within a dormer off the open bunk space of the second floor. The bed could have been placed farther into the dormer, but it's much more interesting—and more fun to play on—with curtains on two sides and a little space between the mattress and the window (practical, too, because its base hides ductwork behind the drawers). The idea for the bed-as-alcove came from Thomas Jefferson's bed at Monticello, a reminder that you can borrow ideas from another period or style and recast them in your own.

Children's bath Two old vanities, relieved of rust and painted yellow, were expertly replumbed and fitted into the children's bath. Placing the two vanities together, along with the twin medicine cabinets, more than doubles the impact.

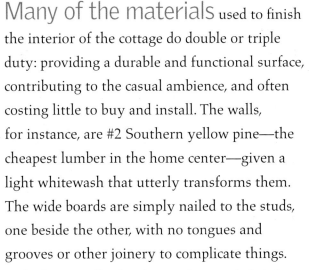

Many of the materials used to finish the interior of the cottage do double or triple duty: providing a durable and functional surface, contributing to the casual ambience, and often costing little to buy and install. The walls, for instance, are #2 Southern yellow pine—the cheapest lumber in the home center—given a light whitewash that utterly transforms them. The wide boards are simply nailed to the studs, one beside the other, with no tongues and grooves or other joinery to complicate things.

Cracks between the boards, which naturally develop as the wood shrinks and expands with the weather, only add character. The floors are treated in a similar fashion. Some are #2 Southern yellow pine, like the walls; these floorboards are painted once, then a second time with a slightly different color, so the color of the first coat will start to show through as the top coat wears. The effect is of an older generation's color choice reasserting itself over time.

Other floors, particularly those in the main living spaces and central stair hall, are reclaimed antique heart pine. Admittedly, they're more expensive than the new yellow pine, but the old planks have been left just as they are, some slightly thicker than others and some with beetle damage, though the worst spots have been patched with new wood. The rough-edged planks were butted together without joinery, painted with a wash, then sanded by hand, buffed, sealed, and waxed. The stair treads have been sanded down in the middle to suggest years of use. It's all very convincing; even the new patches look old.

Upstairs hall The Dutch door (only the top opens) adds a playful touch to the second-floor stair hall. The white curtains swivel to the sides of the window on pivoting rods. Recalling the operable shutters on the porch, swiveling curtains don't block the window when swung open.

With exposed ceiling joists, the structure is the decoration.

<< Even a detail as simple as a stair tread can be made highly expressive.

Plain, polished materials provide an ideal surface for the play of light.

What the mostly white interior gives up in color
it gains back in intensity.

Detailed
for the View

This Rhode Island house sits on a waterfront property on
the East Passage of Narragansett Bay. The site is very long, front to back,
with an unusually narrow waterfront; the most expansive ocean views are
not straight ahead but beyond the southeast corner of the property, a tricky
site on which to build. The owners hired architect Peter Twombly, whose
partner James Estes designed the cottage we looked at on pp. 42–49. Each of
these architects has his own approach to design, though they share a broad
aesthetic. With this house and the cottage on nearby Block
Island, we have an opportunity to see two distinct yet
related ways to detail an honest, straight-ahead house.

Peter oriented the house lengthwise on the site, with
a narrow gable end directly facing the water. The rooms are
arranged lineally, each with ocean views to its south side.
On the waterfront end, the living room and the master
bedroom above also open to the view through corner windows. The placement of the house and its organization are
large design moves and not in themselves details. But at

outside the house

Getting Shelves to Float

The four long, white shelves in the living room (see the bottom left photo on p. 114) were attached to the wall studs with metal brackets before the drywall was installed. The brackets are sandwiched within each shelf,

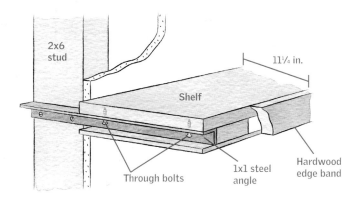

which is constructed like a long box. This is one of several ways to attach shelves to a wall without visible means of support so they appear to float; it looks seamless and highly convincing, but it requires construction ahead of drywall installation (in a remodel, the old drywall would have to be removed first).

every opportunity, Peter has detailed the interior with the linear orientation of the house and its oblique ocean views firmly in mind.

Let's look at the corner windows in the living room.

Especially in this calm space, the corner grouping of two triple windows with transom windows above (the most glass in one place anywhere in the house) all but screams: "The view is over here!" The same is true of the corner windows upstairs in the master bedroom. On the other hand, the little square window in the master bedroom addresses the view in exactly the opposite way, by providing a contained glimpse. Think of it as a square porthole on the bow of a ship.

The linearity of the house is emphasized in the grooved wall below the stairs and, strikingly, in the long floating shelves that guide you into the living room from the entry hall. You probably don't stop to think about the grooves or the shelves, but as you experience the house over time, moving along its length or taking in a long view, these linear elements reinforce the

A WINDOW LIKE A MINIATURE PAINTING The small, square window in the master bedroom acknowledges the center of the house on the exterior, under the oceanside gable, and inside, where it marks the center of the room. The window also lines up with the middle of the corner windows, lending balance and order to the wall opposite the bed. Most of all, the small window offers a framed glimpse in counterpoint to the expansive view offered by the corner windows. Take away the window, and the room becomes much less interesting.

Degrees of separation The half-wall with columns and the steps to either side provide just the right amount of separation between the living room/dining area and the kitchen. The columns mark the width of the kitchen at the center of the house, while space slips easily past them, creating long views and allowing for circulation around—not through—the dining area.

A Staircase Detailed on a Budget

The staircase is the first thing you notice when you step inside; its beguiling geometry animates the entry hall and makes moving through the house a pleasure. Yet this signature element is the result of good design, not great expense.

The curved lower treads embrace the hall the way falling water spreads out after hitting a flat stone. The stair wall has a classic cottage look, though it's surfaced in inexpensive medium-density fiberboard (MDF) scored to look like true tongue-and-groove paneling.

The inexpensive metal spindles were going to be painted white, but they looked better with a clear seal instead. The simple glass blocks capping the newel posts refract light like the old deck lights on a wooden boat; befitting a cottage, they have the quality of sea glass.

Stock cabinet with custom end   To keep costs down, the kitchen cabinets are stock units, but they're spruced up with 2-in.-thick end panels made from maple plywood. The end panels keep you from seeing the toekick reveal in profile, which never looks right. A little of the money saved went toward honed slate countertops, which match the simple elegance of the light maple cabinets.

Study bookshelf The bookshelves in the study are a playful, vertical variation of the floating shelves in the living room. The square window creates a brightly lit display shelf.

A subtle detail The top shelf is set cleanly into the window trim, and the shelf and the trim are the exact same width. This is just the sort of detail we generally don't see and therefore don't request of a builder. And so it gets done wrong. The more you look for such details in well-designed houses, the more you'll see them, and you'll be in a position to ask for them in your own home.

horizontal nature of the house and the site whether you acknowledge them or not.

If linearity and ocean views are two of the larger design issues, another was staying within a reasonable budget. The living room (the owners call it the "not so great room") manages to be the important room in the house without undue expense. It gains additional height not by occupying the roof but by stepping down a foot. It's expensive to build a room with a soaring roof because then you can't build what amounts to relatively cheaper rooms above it. By setting the living-room ceiling at the same height as the ceilings in the rest of the first floor, Peter has

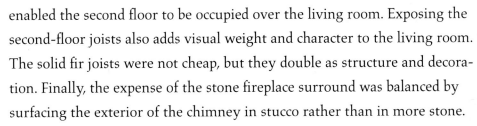

enabled the second floor to be occupied over the living room. Exposing the second-floor joists also adds visual weight and character to the living room. The solid fir joists were not cheap, but they double as structure and decoration. Finally, the expense of the stone fireplace surround was balanced by surfacing the exterior of the chimney in stucco rather than in more stone.

Let's take another look at the Block Island cottage (see pp. 42–49). Where this house comes closest to the cottage is not in any particular material or detail. The real connection lies in the similar way both architects, Peter Twombly and James Estes, approach materials and details, and in their mutual concern for the proportioning of parts, the massing of forms, and the placement of elements. These are big architectural ideas, but in the house shown here, as in the Block Island cottage, big ideas have been brought down to domestic scale. The result, in both cases, is simply a home that makes sense.

Light from below A halogen uplight is a wonderful light fixture for illuminating a ceiling and bouncing reflected light all over a space. With a dimmer switch, you can create a variety of effects, from the ceiling appearing as a bright plane to the ceiling casting the barest warm glow.

Turning a problem into an opportunity Building a house rarely goes without a hitch. In this case, the firebox ended up off center—6 in. farther from the wall than from the built-in media cabinet. The error was reconciled with a few judiciously placed slabs of the same bluestone used for the hearth and mantel. There's more space on the right side of the firebox than on the left, but now the overall stonework composition feels balanced and more interesting. The bluestone rectangle above the mantel is the same size as the rectangular opening at the top of the cabinet, a bit of visual play that brings a smile to your face should you notice it.

A detail in tune with the orientation of the whole Shelves that attach to the wall without brackets or other visible means of vertical support are well suited to a long house on a long site with a long view because we see only their horizontal dimension. Below the floating shelves, a built-up maple plinth carries the line of the bottom stair tread from the hallway.

A trim band set >> roughly at door height keeps tall ceilings from seeming too tall.

^^
When trim is well crafted, even straight lines become highly expressive.

Few materials warm a space as well as orangey woods like fir and cherry.

Craftsman-style details and built-ins add richness to small spaces.

Craftsman Character on a Narrow Lot

Standing up, the human body occupies a spot on the floor roughly 2 ft. by 2 ft., or 4 sq. ft. This mathematical fact doesn't seem to have entered the calculations of people who build houses of 5,000 sq. ft. and 6,000 sq. ft. Just hearing about homes this large skews our sense of scale to the point where we have trouble realizing how little space is required for comfortable living. Forget about these megahouses with their 26-ft. by 46-ft. great rooms and think instead of that virtual 4 sq. ft. surrounding you, because it's the key to realizing how much home you can have in a modest amount of space.

This house in Seattle, Washington, was built in 1905 with 750 sq. ft. on the main floor and 550 sq. ft. upstairs, and even at that size, it's stuffed onto a narrow lot of just 4,000 sq. ft. The owners bought the house as a starter home but became so connected to the neighborhood they decided to stay. Zoning laws prohibited tearing down and rebuilding on the undersized lot; instead, the couple hired architect Gail Wong to add to the house. They wanted more space for

outside the house

Kitchen cabinets These custom-built cherry cabinets have a three-dimensional quality that's hard to achieve with stock cabinetry. If you're in the market for higher-end stock cabinetry, do a little homework; you'll often find that custom-built cabinetry costs the same.

themselves and their young son, but they didn't want to sacrifice too much of their small backyard.

Gail extended the house a mere 14 ft. at the back and reconfigured the roof to create more usable space upstairs. The house now has 2,150 sq. ft. of living space within its narrow confines, and it still doesn't have any large spaces. On the contrary, the new spaces offer testament to the pleasures and functionality of modest dimensions; the primary new space, the family room, is just 10 ft. wide. The addition may be small, but the payoff is big. By choosing to stay in their narrow home on its narrow lot, and by accepting the constraints imposed by a modest addition of space, the owners were able to put their money toward materials, trim, cabinetry, and built-ins that give the formerly nondescript house the warmth and character of a Craftsman-style bungalow.

The Craftsman style is apt for this remodel because

this style, which evolved in the early 20th century, celebrates not only craftsmanship and handwork but also the domestic scale and the comforts of home. For instance, take a look at how the new family room and rejuvenated first floor embody both these aspects of the Craftsman style (see the photos on pp. 122–123). The family room is 23 ft. long, 9 ft. high, and, as already mentioned, just 10 ft. wide. To keep the room from feeling

picture this

THE IMPACT OF A CURVE The curve in this desk embraces the corner as part of the worksurface, and it relieves the linearity of the desk and the space, so this narrow room (you're seeing 90 percent of it) doesn't feel like a mere slot. With the curve removed, you lose its pleasing roundness, and the corner of the desk becomes less usable.

Cherry built-ins The height of the divider between a kitchen and an adjacent space has a huge impact. There's no right or wrong height, just differing degrees of openness and separation. This built-in strikes a nice balance: The upper counter conceals the sink from the family room but allows someone standing to look through.

Half-wall with columns In this second-floor bedroom, a half-wall with columns provides the perfect degree of separation between the bed area and the study area.

uncomfortably tall and narrow, Gail divided it into two areas: a nearly square sitting area that's in line with the original dining room and living room, and a slightly larger rectangular area for an all-purpose table between the kitchen and the back deck. Taking advantage of the tall ceiling, Gail defined each area by a lowered soffit that creates a kind of tray ceiling centered above it.

Each part of the family room features built-ins that enhance the comfort, human scale, and functionality of the entire room. The area with the table features a stunning wall of cherry cabinets (see the left photo on p. 118) that provides a ton of storage and offers views into the kitchen yet maintains a suitable degree of separation. The orange tone of the cherry, the thin muntins dividing the glass cabinet doors, and the many facets of the paneled construction add visual richness to the family room and soften the feel of the space. The sitting area features a deep window seat that's so thoughtfully proportioned and finely detailed it draws you to it from across the house.

If the family room shows what you can do with a space 10 ft. wide, then the window seat shows what's possible in 3 ft. In every way (except in not having a floor), the window seat is treated as a miniature room. It has its own set of windows, of course, but also a mini-library of bookshelves, seating for more than one, a wide sill with room for plants and a reading lamp, and a lowered ceiling framed with wide fir trim.

Master-bath tile A band of decorative tiles (thoughtfully in line with the window frame) breaks up the tiled wall surface. Cutting tiles above and below the band requires a little extra work, but it maintains the centering of the square tiles on the window. Art glass in the lower frame of the window adds visual interest and maintains privacy.

Sizing Up an Informal Eating Booth

This eating booth is sized right for the homeowners who use it every day, but it might not be right for everyone. If you plan to build an eating booth, it's a good idea to try out a few restaurant booths first to discover what feels right. Just bring along a tape measure.

A couple of points to keep in mind: The padded back should have a slight tilt; a ledge or sill behind the top of the seat back, even if it's just a couple of inches wide, gives the booth a more spacious feel; the edge of the seat should overhang the base of the bench, so people can place their feet a little behind their knee; it's usually best if the tabletop overlaps the seat by 4 in. or 5 in. (though the table shown here does not have this overlap); and a table with a center leg makes it easier to get in and out of the booth. If you have extra inches, resist the temptation to make the table or seats too wide—add inches to the sills behind the seats instead.

Master-bedroom window seat The window seat in the master bedroom is the right size for sitting or reclining because it isn't too tall at the edges. Within the triangular form of the dormer, stepped windows provide wall surface for two sconces, which do a better job of providing light for reading than overhead lights.

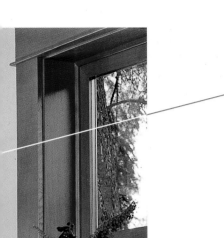

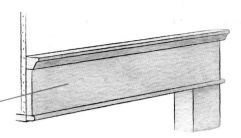

Classic Craftsman-style trim The trim around the window seat is straightforward, honest, and expressive. It has just two pieces that are not absolutely necessary: the crown molding across the top and the narrow spline just above the opening. The crown molding and the spline combine with the wide top trim piece (like a bare-bones Greek frieze) to give the whole framed composition greater weight at the top, an arrangement that has felt right for more than 2,000 years.

The ultimate window seat This window seat is the whole nine yards: wide enough (and cushioned enough) to be a daybed, built of rich cherry, with drawers below and four well-proportioned windows above. But what really sets it apart are a couple of thoughtful details. The wide sill that wraps around the seat provides a place to rest a book or a cup of coffee and keeps your head from bumping against the wall; the bookcases on either side don't hold a lot of books but add immeasurably to the cozy feel; and the gently sloped trim at the front offers a bit of extra containment, lending the window seat the snugness of a boat.

A simple but dignified hearth There's nothing complicated or ornate about this fireplace surround. Its two materials, cherry wood and green limestone, are unadorned save for the angled Shaker-style crown molding across the top. The pleasure is in the thoughtful proportions and in the materials themselves, the warm grain of the cherry and the mottled patina of the limestone.

A shelf of books compels the curiosity seeker in us to walk toward it. ∨

A roof overhang carries >> the ceiling plane outside, extending interior space.

∧ The best way to experience a really thick wall is to pass along its full depth.

Light and space, encouraged by thoughtful details, connect inside to outside.

Rooms Afloat above a Garden

An active gardener in Manchester, Massachusetts, Olga asked architects Gitta Robinson and Richard Grisaru for a home that responded to her passion in two ways: She wanted large expanses of glass and ample doorways that would allow her to enjoy the garden, and she needed a place to keep her growing collection of houseplants, as well as potted plants that have to be brought indoors during the winter.

The steep site suggested tucking a garage, mudroom, and office under the main level, and this lower walkout basement level establishes the main floor a little above grade. From the upper garden side, the house appears to never quite touch the ground. Outside, the architects accentuated the house's light touch on the land with wide roof overhangs and a long wooden deck that extends over a garden pool. Inside, they established a floating, almost weightless, quality with ample openings between adjacent rooms, a layout that lets in lots of bright daylight, and a series of details that cantilever and in some cases appear to hover above the floor.

outside the house

A sign of lightness to come One of the first things you see upon entering the house is the gap in the corner between two translucent panels that serve as stair rails. You may not consciously notice the open corner, but your mind likely registers the idea of openness it signals, subtly setting you up to experience the lightness and airiness of the entire house.

Purple Sliders

The purple doors that slide out from either side of the hearth aren't pulled open often, but when they are, they make a real statement. The doors also enable the library (which has its own full bath) to be used as a guest bedroom or, in the future, as a main-floor master bedroom. The firebox has been painted with heat-resistant black paint, which looks much less new and stark than white firebrick.

A perfect example of a detail that floats is the hearthstone, a polished concrete slab that extends from the chimney mass like a thick shelf, 15 in. above the floor. You feel the full weight of the hearthstone, visibly spanning as it does the length and breadth of the chimney into which it is pinned, and yet it hovers. Space flows under the hearthstone just as it flows under the wooden deck outside.

In a slightly less literal way, the entire chimney is an object floating in the middle of a long space, dividing the living-room side from the library side. It's an artful composition in its own right and an illustration of the Not So Big concept of useful beauty. The chimney mass is not simply a sculptural object. It's a wall that divides two spaces, a sound buffer, a fireplace, a media center, an impromptu seat, a display area, a surface that reflects natural and artificial light into the rooms, and a place to conceal two large pocket doors; it's even a place for storing firewood.

Take a close look at the chimney in the photo at left. All of its parts have been considered and arranged with great care, yet in a way that ends up looking effortless. A firebox is typically placed slap-bang in the middle of the chimney, but it doesn't have to be. By placing the firebox to one side, Gitta and Richard allowed the white wall (plaster over concrete block, in this case) to become a blank canvas

Entry and landing The second step from the entry to the stair hall extends along the side wall, combining with the picture frame to make the artwork on the wall seem more important.

for whatever is displayed in front of it. Placing the firebox to one side also leaves space behind the blank wall for the firewood niche. Gitta and Richard take a similar approach with the cherry media cabinet that is set into its own niche within the chimney mass to the left of the firebox. The hearth-stone would be a logical place for the bottom of the cabinet, but instead the cabinet hovers above it, again reinforcing the floating theme and also creating a display area on the hearthstone.

Along with the media cabinet, most of the wood elements throughout the house, whether of cherry or oak, satisfy the definition of useful beauty,

Conservatory The fixed-glass window in the stone-tiled plant conservatory (at the far end of the stair hall) takes up the entire wall and is minimally detailed to feel almost as if it isn't there. Glass panels in the floor allow light to reach the mudroom on the lower level and appear with the plants as little reflecting pools, blurring the distinction between the conservatory and the garden.

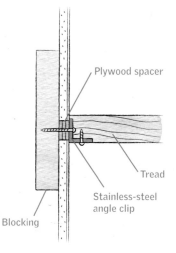

---

the way it's done

Floating Stair Treads

Many people love the buoyant, weightless look of open stairs, which have solid treads but no risers. It's more difficult to build open stairs now that the maximum allowable gap in any part of a stairway has been reduced to 4 in. One trick I've employed is to add a strip of wood underneath each tread, recessed from the edge to decrease the gap between the treads without overly increasing their apparent thickness. But how to attach the "floating" treads to the walls? On this stair, metal clips are recessed into each end of these treads, one of the least obtrusive of several options.

Plywood spacer

Tread

Stainless-steel angle clip

Blocking

Library ladder A simple but elegant handcrafted oak ladder is all it takes to make what is otherwise a room with a long bookshelf feel more like a proper library. The ladder rungs and the handholds lend a tactile quality to the room, as do the books, of course.

providing storage or some other function while also adding warmth and texture. In an interior as white and brightly lit as this one, wood is an ideal accent material. Given the linear nature of wood, it's no surprise that many of the floating details—the stair treads, for instance, or the breakfast-nook seats—are made of wood; these, too, embody useful beauty. And it would be hard to imagine a more straightforward expression of useful beauty than the handcrafted oak ladder in the library.

Breakfast nook The breakfast nook feels like a place of its own because it's defined by the corner windows. Even with a deck just beyond the windows, this corner spot feels perched above the garden outside. The near seat is cantilevered, another variation on the theme of lightness and floating.

Low shelves Low bookshelves run the length of the west wall beneath windows to the garden. The long shelves slip past the hearth to connect the library to the living room. Light from the glass door at the far end of the library draws you toward the garden just outside.

The house contains many details and elements that subtly appear to defy gravity, but the sense of buoyancy one feels in this interior is arguably affected most by the quality of light. The house has been oriented so that the kitchen and dining room face south, which makes these two heavily used spaces very bright on sunny days. The windows in the living room and library face east and west, so the light there shifts across the hours of the day. The stair hall, with its tall wall of glass, serves as a kind of light bridge connecting the living room/library and the dining room/kitchen.

But the form and orientation of the house are not the only reasons the interior feels so airy. The spaces also feel open because they're made up of elements that allow light to pass through them. Of course, the windows and glass doors let light in from outside. But once inside, the light continues to flow, through the openings between the stair treads, through the translucent stair panels, through the glass doors of the cabinet between the kitchen and dining room, and through glass panels set into the conservatory floor. Light and space are rather similar in the way they flow, and in this house, it's both light and space, encouraged by thoughtful details, that connect inside to outside even as the house floats above the garden.

A not-quite-see-through cabinet The display cabinet suspended between the kitchen and the dining room dances on the line between openness and containment. Its thin glass shelves, lit from within, and the slim reveal that ever-so-slightly separates the door frames from the ceiling give the cabinet a floating quality. Clear glass on the kitchen side lets you see the glassware displayed within; translucent glass on the dining-room side dampens the impact of the glassware, creating a slightly more formal, less cluttered feel.

Sizing a sink window The way the window behind the sink comes to rest flush with the countertop is an elegant detail, but it's one that requires some forethought. Assuming you want the tops of all the windows to line up, you need a window that fits exactly between the head of the rough opening and the countertop. Few stock windows do. Rather than spend money on a custom window, I often use a stock window behind the sink to set the head height of all the windows in the house.

Cut-out cabinet corner
Stopping the lower cabinets short of the end of the countertop softens the look of the corner and lets the countertop overhang just enough to read as though it's floating, a theme repeated throughout the interior.

<< A lowered ceiling plane adds intimacy to the area below it.

Space appears >> to flow more freely when it has an object to move around.

<< Distinctive materials distinguish special elements from their surroundings.

Opening up the house makes an ordinary ranch more livable . . .
and more beautiful.

A Modest Ranch Opens Up

Steve and Courtney's ongoing ranch remodel in Atlanta has been a labor of love since the couple bought the house in 1998. Built in the 1960s, the understated 2,100-sq.-ft. ranch had good lines and enough space for the family of four; it simply needed updating. From the beginning, Steve and Courtney knew they wanted "better not bigger space." By adding just 80 sq. ft. to the kitchen, and through a combination of small moves inside, Steve, an architect, created a surprisingly sophisticated ensemble of interior spaces. The room functions remain where they had been in the original, but now the spaces themselves overlap each other. Opening up the house involved judiciously removing some of the long wall at the center, varying the height of the ceilings, and adding furniturelike components, such as a breakfast booth, a tall display cabinet, a round worktable, and media cabinets. These built-in details (mostly of cherry, though the round table is beech) combine with carefully controlled natural and artificial light

outside the house

A Cabinet That Does Double Duty

This cherry cabinet provides storage and a display area while also serving as the back of the breakfast nook. Its Masonite panel doors are just right for kid art. There are square piers on either side of the cabinet; one stops below the floating ceiling, an expression of support, but the other continues past the ceiling, stopping just slightly above it, a playful way to emphasize the sculptural qualities of both the ceiling and the cabinet.

and custom-sized rugs to define distinct functional areas while letting space flow.

In the original ranch, the interior was divided right down the middle by a structural wall that supported the ceiling joists at their centers. With just two doors through it, the wall effectively cut off views and the flow of space from one side of the house to the other. To bring the rooms together, Steve opened the wall between the family room and living room and widened the opening between the kitchen and dining room. The fairly long central wall that remains now reads as a distinct object within the interior. It's a thick plane with space flowing around it, no longer a wall with doorways piercing through it. The central white wall adds reflected light to the rooms on both sides and serves, with the other white walls, as backdrop for the worktable, media cabinets, and other wood elements.

Along with the central wall, the ceilings have been redefined

to create spatial zones rather than distinct rooms. It's the variation in ceiling height, more than the walls, that tells you you're in a particular area of the interior. In the kitchen addition, the ceiling vaults upward in the opposite direction to the original roof, creating a brightly lit clerestory area above the whole expanded kitchen. To take advantage of the additional light and to tie the kitchen and family room closely together, the family-room ceiling has been opened up to the original roofline, vaulting up to the central wall. Light from the clerestory windows now illuminates the family room as well as the kitchen. On the other side of the central wall, the flat ceiling has been maintained at its original height. The change in the ceiling from vaulted to flat helps to differentiate the family room from the living room.

Media cabinet detail
There's nothing fussy about the built-in media cabinet. Because of its recessed base and the lack of a solid corner, the cabinet appears to hover just above the floor, reinforcing your sense that space is flowing freely within the interior.

The drama of a lowered ceiling plane

Though it's a relatively simple detail, the lowered ceiling plane achieves many things at once. By spanning the entire width of the house, it stitches together the spaces on either side of the central wall; it allows you to experience the wood accent wall and the wood display cabinet as bookends, further linking the two sides; and it helps define the dining area, the breakfast booth, and a sink work area. Finally, the floating section frames views between the family room and kitchen and from the kitchen into the family room.

Objects in space

The wall that divides the living room and family room feels like a plane in space because of its apparent thickness and because it meets the ceiling without any trim. There's no framed doorway between the two rooms, just free-flowing space. The hub of the house is the round, built-in table that continues as a media cabinet along the central wall. The table, like the wall, appears as a sculptural object, but it's differentiated from the wall as well as from space around it by its warm color and rounded shape.

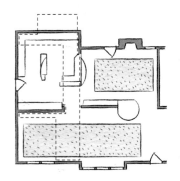

Delineating activity areas underfoot

A long rug, designed and made for the house, defines a sitting area in both the living room and the dining area; on the other side of the wall, a more compact custom rug defines a family-room sitting area. The rugs run perpendicular to the floating ceiling plane, creating a kind of plaid effect, a stitching together of space similarly explored by Frank Lloyd Wright. The rugs have bold stripes and squares that relate from one rug to the other, a subtle way to unify the rooms.

A soffit lends the hearth intimacy The soffit extends beyond the chimney and across the window, tying the chimney and window together in a balanced composition. It's the perfect surface on which to locate two spotlights for illuminating artwork on the mantel.

A well-defined kitchen The kitchen reads as a smaller, contained space within the large, open space of the overall interior, rather than as a discrete room. The floating ceiling and the degree of openness contribute to this effect, as does the wood half-wall and cabinetry, which together define the kitchen as a distinct entity.

The most striking ceiling innovation is a lowered horizontal plane that begins outside as a trellis extending beyond the kitchen addition and then carries through the kitchen as a free-floating plane, defining an intimate breakfast booth below it. The plane rests on a display cabinet, then slips through the central wall and becomes a lowered (though no longer floating) ceiling defining the dining area from the slightly taller living room to one side and the slightly taller family music area to the other.

This horizontal ceiling plane is a great example of a detail that does double duty, defining distinct areas of space below it and animating the whole interior. Take a look at the photo on p. 139, and you can almost feel the ceiling plane thrust through the central spine of the house. It's the physical embodiment of spatial flow.

Window treatments

Although they're closely connected, the living room and the dining room each have their own character because of the way their windows have been treated. Set high, the dining-room windows provide light and also containment, so dining doesn't become a public display. The casual living room is defined by its bay of floor-to-ceiling windows.

Kitchen island Though it is quite functional, the kitchen island is the most purely sculptural of the wood built-ins within the interior. The top is for working on, but because it's transparent glass, your eye rests on the curve of the thick cherry shelf, a mirror of the curved countertop between the kitchen and family room.

Local materials, by their nature, help connect a house to its surroundings.

A corner window >> makes you believe the room ends outside, in the distance.

<< Diagonal views stretch space across the longest dimension of a room.

This split-level ranch remodel feels at one with its forest setting.

The Nature of Materials

It's wonderful when a house is so thoroughly rooted in the land that it becomes an integral part of its surroundings. Sadly, too few houses are built with this kind of sensitivity, and a remodel isn't likely to create a connection to the land that didn't exist in the first place. But you might be surprised by how many older houses have a latent sense of place, buried under years of outmoded styling and bad decisions, just waiting for someone to come along and make it manifest.

If you had seen the 1960s rambler Andy and Rose bought in Bellevue, Washington, before its transformation, you'd never have guessed it had the bones of a forest house. It looked like a split-level ranch that could be in any suburb anywhere, not like a house set deep in the woods. Inside, the house was dark and dreary, divided down the middle by a white stone fireplace and indoor barbeque, with cavelike rooms further divided by the awkward split-level design. Outside, the house was a long, white box that sliced through the treed landscape in an unsettled way.

outside the house

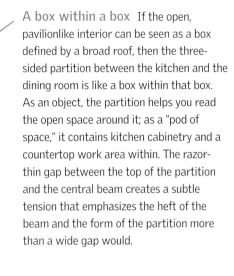

A box within a box If the open, pavilionlike interior can be seen as a box defined by a broad roof, then the three-sided partition between the kitchen and the dining room is like a box within that box. As an object, the partition helps you read the open space around it; as a "pod of space," it contains kitchen cabinetry and a countertop work area within. The razor-thin gap between the top of the partition and the central beam creates a subtle tension that emphasizes the heft of the beam and the form of the partition more than a wide gap would.

Materials that express themselves naturally The interior is unified by natural materials that echo the earthy tones of the surrounding forest. Although the materials are clearly related by the colors and hues of nature, each also expresses the unique qualities of its own nature: Glass is glass, wood is wood, and stone is stone. This might seem a given, but often we treat materials in ways that contradict their true nature, and when we do that, even local, natural materials can lose their sense of place.

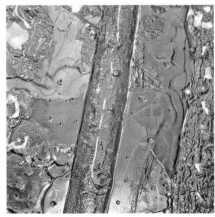

Stairs to office The open corner of the upper-level home office and the stair railings resolve the split of the split-level floor plan, visually connecting the office to the main level. The office feels a bit like a loft; it's possible to focus on work there and yet not feel removed from the family life below.

Andy and Rose first approached architect and design-builder Julie Campbell for a new roof and windows, but Julie quickly convinced them that with a thorough remodeling the house had the potential to be a bright, open pavilion in the woods. Julie extended the roof overhangs, created porches and decks, and replaced the roofing, windows, and siding with materials whose textures, colors, and forms befit the landscape. Sliding glass doors, skylights, and corner windows were added; a glass-covered canopy was built above the entry; and the dining-room wall was repositioned farther under the roof, creating a narrow veranda that feels like a Japanese *engawa*. The house now appears as a contemporary cross between a Japanese house and the traditional longhouse of the indigenous Northwest Coast peoples.

The original house had a huge fir beam at the center of the main level, with smaller but still substantial beams resting on it and in turn supporting a ceiling of fir boards, but all of this had been painted white or was concealed by interior walls. The first order of business was to strip off the paint so that the roof overhead would recover its Northwest character. To open up the main level and further emphasize the sheltering roof, the central chimney and all the walls were removed. A stone chimney was built on an exterior wall of the living room, and the interior walls were replaced with partitions that stop short of the ceiling, so you experience the full sweep of the roof.

picture this

LESS IS MORE One of the discoveries made during remodeling was that the central fir beam ended at the entry area. An obvious response would have been to continue the beam by butting another beam to it. But by accentuating the end of the beam on top of the tree-trunk column, the heft of the beam becomes stunningly apparent, and the openness of the ceiling above it is maintained. Extending the beam is not a bad idea, as you can see, but it's far less dramatic than exposing its end grain.

A unified interior There's considerable textural variety and spatial complexity in the open interior, and yet there is also a cohesive quality to the whole. The dominant roof unifies the space underneath it, and complementary colors, mostly of a warm, orangey hue, pull together materials of varying texture. The repetition of black details—brackets, tiles, countertop, fireplace surround, light fixtures—further unifies the look of the interior.

The kitchen is defined by a translucent glass panel that's clipped to the ceiling and by a boxlike partition that functions as a "pod of space" (see the photo on pp. 144–145). This pod contains cabinetry on the kitchen side and provides a wall surface on the dining-room side for a large painting. The coat closet is also a pod of space, providing storage at the entry area and defining one corner of the living room. All of the materials—from the kitchen wall tiles to the fireplace stonework to the fir cabinetry—have an earthy feel that ties them to the outdoors. Even the glass panel has an outdoor connection in its patterned imprint of trees and plants found on the property.

To speak separately of changes outside and changes inside is to misrepresent the house, because the real change has been in the blurring of indoors and out. Especially in the entry sequence, Julie has taken a very

detail in focus

The Interplay of Stone and Wood

One of the best ways to express the nature of one material is to place it in contrast with a second material. Interspersing square slate tiles and lengths of oak floorboards heightens our appreciation of the qualities of each material. This particular effect requires the careful work of an expert flooring installer, but the interplay of stone and wood gently grabs our attention even as it eases the transition from the slate terrace outside to the wood entry area inside.

Home office A clerestory window above the stairs throws light into the office and hallway. In a typical split-level, you feel you might hit your head on the ceiling each time you start down from the top of the stairs. Here, the stairs begin well away from the wall, and the clerestory eliminates the feeling that you're walking right at something solid.

Entry sequence The melding of indoors and out is marvelously expressed in the entry sequence, which begins under a glass-covered canopy supported by two colossal tree-trunk columns. The slate pavers of the terrace continue into the house, passing through the doorway without the interruption of a threshold—a subtle but powerful detail. The sequence ends with another colossal fir column.

Japanese approach to easing the indoor-outdoor transition. The most prominent element of the interior is the thick trunk of a Douglas fir, stripped of its bark, that supports the central beam and defines the far inside corner of the entry. This natural fir column mirrors two similar tree-trunk columns holding up the glass-covered canopy above the entry terrace outside. And all three fir columns mimic the tall firs growing on the property. The indoor-outdoor transition is also softened at the floor level. The grid pattern of slate pavers covering the outdoor entry terrace moves seamlessly inside but then breaks down one tile at a time to mesh with the wood flooring.

In the original house, there was almost no connection between the main level and either the lower or upper levels. Now when Andy or Rose or their young daughter stands at the top of the upper-level stairs, they see down through rails into the open main level and out through a clerestory window to the stone chimney and the trees beyond. From the very spot where the house had been the darkest and most disconnected, it's now possible to experience a broad sense of unity.

<< Tracing a line of trim allows us to experience the three-dimensionality of space.

Thin window muntins >> add human scale without diminishing openness.

A hall made wide and filled with light becomes a room to spend time in.

Trim creates contrast as well as continuity.

Simple Trim, Substantial Impact

Sharon and Brett's house in Asheville, North Carolina, was built new, but it presents a perfect opportunity to talk about traditional home details and why people like them. Architect Jim Samsel honored the couple's request for a house with the character of their previous home, a Craftsman-style bungalow they'd restored in Atlanta. As Jim took cues from the land, the new house evolved from a bungalow into a mountain cottage, still with Craftsman-style trim and details inside, but now with a cruciform plan that neatly fits both the site and Sharon and Brett's requirements. You get a sense of the cruciform shape when approaching the projecting front of the house, but the real impact is felt when you step inside. A cruciform is admirably suited to a Not So Big House because it enables small rooms projecting from the center each to have windows on two or three sides, creating spacious-ness without undue square footage.

Upon entering, the first thing you notice is the pleasant contrast established by the dark trim against the white walls.

outside the house

A fine balance You don't have to divide an entire window to get the impact of divided panes. With thin muntins dividing just the top quarter of each sash, these casement windows strike a balance between the openness of contemporary undivided windows and the sheltering quality of traditional divided windows. The muntins also keep these windows from feeling too tall.

The trim is stained Southern yellow pine, but it looks like rich oak. The impact of the trim is amplified by its width—7¼ in. for the baseboards and 5½ in. for the crown molding and the head trim above the windows— and also by the consistent way the trim has been applied from room to room. Trim of a contrasting color to the walls adds visual punch and, more significantly, differentiates the various parts of the interior—floors, windows, doors, walls—from each other, thereby creating visual complexity.

At the same time the trim creates contrast, it also creates continuity. The constancy of the trim ties the spaces together. The color and material of the trim stitch together the floor, cabinets, windows,

and doors (all are of similar hue if not always of the same wood). The lines of the trim pull together the furnishings, especially the Craftsman-style and Mission-style chairs, sofas, and tables, in whose own lines and colors the trim is echoed. The trim in this house is doing a lot of work, even though it's not ornate or

detail in focus

Rhythm of the Rails

Stair rails are too often spaced the minimum 4 in. apart, which doesn't always look good. Here a simple rhythm has been established: three rails really close together, then a gap, then three rails, and so on. Although the rails themselves are nothing fancy—just 2x2 pine— their thoughtful placement adds character to the stair hall (as does the graceful wall niche).

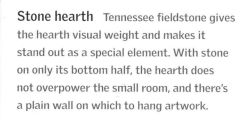

Stone hearth Tennessee fieldstone gives the hearth visual weight and makes it stand out as a special element. With stone on only its bottom half, the hearth does not overpower the small room, and there's a plain wall on which to hang artwork.

Display cabinets add useful beauty Small cabinets with glass doors add display space for items used only on occasion. The storage cabinets would have looked too tall if they had run uninterrupted to the ceiling, and the top shelves would have been difficult to reach. In this interior, where the full ceiling height has been maintained throughout, soffits would have looked out of place.

Harmony on a small scale Although the sink area is composed of a number of different materials—wood, tile, and solid-surface countertop—the overall effect is harmonious. The sink and countertop are a single unit, with no seams to keep clean, and yet the white sink set within the green stonelike counter surface feels like an old-fashioned farmhouse sink.

Slender French doors There's a delightful slimness to the trim and other interior elements that's in tune with the 10-ft. height of the rooms. The exterior doorway in the dining area (to the right of the photo on the facing page) is a narrow 4 ft. wide and a tall 8 ft. high. Each of the French doors, therefore, is unusually narrow, with panes divided by slim horizontal muntins to emphasize the vertical. Thinness and linearity are further accentuated by a slim groove cut into the face of the wood door frame, visible in the photo at far right.

Dividing a wall with a chair rail Chair rails were originally meant to keep chair backs from damaging the plaster, but a rail makes sense simply to bring down the apparent height of a wall and add character to a room. This rail is a nicely stained but otherwise unadorned 1x2 strip of pine, set 36 in. from the floor, even with the countertop, which continues the line into the kitchen.

complicated. Not surprisingly, the blandness of today's stock houses is often partly the result of a lack of trim.

Why is it that even simple trim evokes such strong feelings of domesticity? We respond first to the visual effect of trim. Trim relates to our hands, and our hands in turn to our sense of scale. Looking at trim, you can imagine your hand running along it, you can figure the size of the things trimmed. And in this house, where the trim material is a richly stained oak, you respond further to the natural warmth of wood. You might not think consciously about any of this, but you feel it all the same.

Interior window A small interior window adds interest to the stairwell as well as to the desk alcove in the home office on the other side.

The chair rail continues For scale and consistency, the chair rail that figures prominently in the dining area continues in the kitchen area, even where there's just a few inches of wall. Maintaining the chair rail helps you read the kitchen area and the dining area as one larger space.

A CONTINUOUS BAND OF TILE This master bath presents a contemporary take on the old-fashioned look of white tile. In a more traditional bath, the black trim tile would have stopped at the wood window trim. Here, the tile band continues around the window (and then around the double windows over the tub), strengthening the impact of the window. Stop the trim at the window, and the whole room becomes less interesting. Centering the towel bar (and the floor register) on the window heightens the impact.

Details in the trim Though the trim in this house is exceedingly simple, it's not without subtle embellishment. The head trim above the doors and windows is a touch wider and thicker than the side trim, and it protrudes beyond the side trim, weighting the top ever so slightly. The trim at the base of the doorjambs and posts is just a little thicker than the baseboard, creating a reveal.

While the trim and wood details lend Sharon and

Brett's home a traditional air, the floor plan gives it a modern quality of openness and flow. The kitchen and dining areas are essentially one room, though subtle cues define one area from the other: for instance, the positioning of the sink counter in a bay that protrudes beyond the dining room. The most pronounced sense of openness, surprisingly, is at the very center of the cruciform plan, which typically feels hemmed in by the rooms springing from it. In Sharon and Brett's house, what begins as a stone-floored front hall expands into a wide gallery for displaying artwork.

The gallery, not the trim, may be the real secret to the domestic quality of the house. In the end, the trim works so well because the spaces themselves work so well, which is why merely adding trim to an ill-conceived house rarely creates the kind of place you see here.

Substantial trim can make an ordinary wall feel more consequential.

<< In a very small house, a little layering of space goes a long way.

An opening in a >> thick wall is a great place to tuck in a little storage.

The details are what make this tiny apartment a joy to live in.

Grace, Elegance, and Storage—in 650 sq. ft.

This one-bedroom apartment in a 1908 Beaux Arts building in Washington, D.C., first belonged to Gail, an architect, whose plans for her modest 650-sq.-ft. home were fully realized only after she met and later married Tom, a builder. Ten years after Gail bought a most ordinary apartment, it's now an extraordinary—and extraordinarily compact—example of carefully established interior views, double-duty elements, well-proportioned spaces, and clever storage, all of it detailed with imaginative colors and richly built-up trim that takes advantage of the apartment's thick walls and high ceilings. The classical trim ties the apartment to the elegant, heavily corniced exterior of the building and to the historic neighborhood. But more than that, the details are what make the apartment a joy to live in.

Design is a process that frequently begins as a conversation, a discussion of possibilities around the table, maybe even a polite argument or two. This is how it was for Gail and Tom. Confronted with a bath, bedroom, living room,

outside the house

Foyer Paneling and an unanticipated yet pleasing pale orange wall add warmth and dignity to this tiny foyer. The value of the orange color sets up the yellow of the living room; the paneling announces the character of the apartment; and the painting, lit from above, gives the person entering the comfort of having some light to walk toward.

and kitchen, lined up just like that, they considered removing the wall between the living room and kitchen entirely, making at least one big, open space. But where to put the washer and dryer? The design Gail and Tom arrived at—think of it as a single, grand detail—solved the washer and dryer problem *and* supplied a feeling of spaciousness. It also made the kitchen work much better and created a new space of sorts, a virtual dining room.

What had been a wall with a door between the living room and kitchen has become a paneled opening that is 10 ft. wide and 34 in. deep, exactly the width of the dining table that rests against one side of the opening. The table acts as a room divider, defining the edge of the living room on one side and the edge of the kitchen on the other. The top panels of the opening, which are several inches lower than the ceiling in the rooms to either side, define a transitional space that, in effect, is a dining room, albeit a very narrow one. At night, with lights dimmed in the kitchen and living room, the two lights hanging above the table reinforce the sense that you're sitting in a distinct dining space.

The dining table, it turns out, is not what determined the width of the paneled opening. Rather, the width was set by the closetlike pantries on either side of the opening. Gail and Tom decided to put the dryer inside the inner pantry and the washer in the pantry next to the exterior wall, where it had to be for plumbing reasons. The space above the opening houses the dryer vent on its run to the exterior wall. There's a slight inconvenience to

Taking Cues from What's Already There

The original transom window above the door to the bathroom provided a cue to detailing the rest of the space. To keep the tiny room from feeling too tall, wainscoting was added to the height of the door, its trim line giving your eye a place to rest below the full ceiling height, thus making the space seem lower. A second transom window was added over the tub, creating an enclosed bathing nook. The thick wall of the bath was used to store and hang towels, but for visual continuity, the trim line above the wainscoting was maintained across the towel niche.

Galley kitchen In this foreshortened view, you can see how the dining table, set into the wide opening to the living room, maintains the former edge of the galley kitchen without making the kitchen feel narrow and cramped, as it did when there was a wall in place of the opening.

Color and pattern details The detailing of this apartment carries down to the smallest color, pattern, and material choices, every one of them an opportunity to contribute to the overall feel of the home. For example, the squares of the slate tile kitchen backsplash are picked up in the living-room pillows and also in the rug in the foyer. Likewise, nickel drawer pulls are used on the kitchen cabinets and again in the dressing room.

having the dryer separate from the washer, rather than stacked, but now there's twice the usable countertop surface, one countertop above each appliance.

Storage is tucked everywhere in this little apartment:

under the window in the kitchen, within the thick wall of the bath, in the hall leading to the bedroom. The living room felt too long, so Gail and Tom shortened it by building in a bookshelf at one end and cabinets under the windows at the other end, thus adding storage and improving the proportions of the room without affecting its functionality.

As is often the case, storage goes hand in hand with trim, simply because cabinets, closet doors, and shelving create lots of edges and openings to be trimmed, making the plain walls of the original apartment more useful and visually interesting. Throughout the apartment, raised panels and

picture this

THE IMPORTANCE OF BEING PANELED
The paneling in this apartment bedroom adds visual interest while reflecting light from the two windows. Remove the paneling, and the bay window effect is less pronounced; the wall and the room become more ordinary (though a painting on the bare wall would help).

What to Do with a Flat-Screen TV

You can hang a flat-screen TV on a wall, of course, but here's an option for setting one into a bookshelf. The TV screen is mounted on a fabric-covered sheet of Homasote®, a paper-based fiberboard. The sheet, with holes cut in it for speakers, is set halfway into the shelf, leaving space behind it for the speakers themselves and wiring (and, in this case, a TV tuner, since the screen is just a monitor).

paneled cabinet doors are used to break up the surface of the walls. In the wide doorway from foyer to living room, the panels are cabinet doors, opened by touch latches rather than door pulls. Here the trim *is* the storage (or at least the access to it).

In an old house, nothing lines up, floors dip, walls are out of plumb. Trim is a great way to add impact and at the same time deal with the imperfections of construction, time, or both. In a modern house with little or no trim, on the other hand, materials have to come together perfectly; everything has to fit just right; lines have to be straight and edges crisp. In this traditional space, trim cleans up the mess and becomes a key characteristic of the apartment's personality.

Pantries on either side There are two pantries in the kitchen, one on either side of the big opening. The left pantry has a washing machine below a usable countertop, plus space for a food processor and mixer. The dryer is in the right pantry, along with a second countertop and space for a microwave, toaster oven, and coffee maker.

Storage, storage everywhere This is a good example of getting more by giving up just a little floor space. Cabinets under the windows add storage and a display area while shortening the otherwise long room, improving its proportions. The wall has been made to appear like a large bay window by angling the corners. The built-out corners hide heating pipes and provide room for built-in stereo speakers.

Hidden storage A deep closet in the dressing area down the hall has been treated like a pantry, with hinged shelves that swing out to reveal more storage behind.

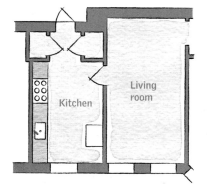

Opening up—but not all the way
In place of a wall between the living room and kitchen, a wide opening defines a narrow zone of space for the dining table and for pantries to either side of the opening. The dining table divides the living room from the kitchen while allowing a strong visual connection between the spaces. Getting rid of the wall entirely would have created one large room but no distinct place for the dining table and no pantries.

A little metal, by way of >> contrast, brings out the warmth of wood.

Four-foot-six is >> a nice width for an opening, neither too big nor too small.

^^
A movable interior element literally puts people in touch with a home.

166

A few key details tie the rooms together and create a unity of effect.

Rooms Defined but Not Confined

What began as a nondescript 1960s house, something of a sore thumb on a boulevard of elegant 1920s homes, has been transformed into a house that befits its well-established Minneapolis neighborhood. From the start, homeowners Beth and Rick opted for high-quality materials rather than an overabundance of space, a Not So Big approach gladly embraced by architect Jean Rehkamp Larson.

Remodeling meant gutting the entire interior of the house and then adding space at the back for a kitchen, family room, and mudroom. Jean cleverly placed the front hall, mudroom, stairs, and powder room all on one side, creating privacy there and freeing up the main spaces front to back so they could more easily connect to each other. Where a smidgen of extra space was needed on the sides, Jean bumped out rooms or alcoves just a foot or two beyond the original walls. Within the house, she allowed the spaces to open to one another without losing their identity as individual rooms. As Jean puts it, the rooms are "defined but not confined."

outside the house

A kitchen window mini-bay You don't need thick walls to enjoy wide windowsills. As you can see from inside and outside, these corner windows are part of a slim bay that juts beyond the wall 6 in., just enough to allow for a wide sill above the sink and countertop.

Degrees of separation You have choices about how much or little the wall divides two spaces. A partial wall can feel like a true wall with holes punched in it, like columns, or like built-in furniture. To divide this kitchen and family room, the architect considered cabinetry alone—which would have made the two spaces feel more like one big kitchen—but settled on a combination of wall-like piers and a counter-height wood cabinet, with a thick shelf above. The shelf's metal support rods echo those above the dining-room interior windows.

The delight of an unexpected detail The main countertop of the kitchen island is in line with the countertops and the partial wall. The small lower countertop, supported by brackets but otherwise suspended from the island, offers a bit of a twist. It has its own logic, being just the right height for pulling up a chair instead of a stool.

Throwing in a Curve

You don't have to have tall ceilings to vary their height. The curved ceiling that's been added within this short, 8-ft.-high hallway takes away a few inches of headroom yet heightens the sense of transition between the front entry and the mudroom (the interior window throws a little light into the stairs to the basement). The dark cherry paneling accentuates the shape of the curve and distinguishes it from the regular flat ceilings.

Mudroom alcove The alcove added to this existing mudroom contributes to its usefulness and its character. The bench offers an opportunity for some color and a place to sit; the cherry cabinets augment an existing closet and warm up the look of the room; and the windows bring in natural light. Like the window seat upstairs, the alcove is cantilevered from the existing house structure and does not require a foundation.

Front hall Throughout the house, metal is used as an accent to the more dominant wood trim and paneling. The stainless-steel rails liven up the look of the stairs yet complement the blond maple and red cherry wood. You won't find metalwork like this at a home center, but a good architect can design it for you and have it made to order by a local fabricator.

Keeping the rooms small and discrete means there are no huge spaces in the house. On the other hand, it's by encountering a series of spaces that you get to enjoy the expansive effects of layering. *Layering* may sound like an obscure architectural notion, but it's simply a word used to describe the very tangible experience of being in one space while seeing into and through other spaces. And it's the details as much as the rooms themselves that sustain the illusion of more space than is actually there. The sliding windows between the dining room and the eating area of the kitchen are a perfect example of a detail that creates a layering effect. Look at the left photo on p. 172. The family room, seen through a wide, unframed opening, seems really close, almost part of the dining room. But looking past or through the window frames, you have a restricted view of the eating area and a mere glimpse of the kitchen; you feel there is more space beyond the windows to explore, perhaps to arrive at later. In this way, layering creates interest—even intrigue—as well as spaciousness.

At the same time, a few key details tie the rooms together and create a unity of effect, a sense that no matter which room you're in, you're still in the same house. The most prominent continuous details

Look at the left photo on p. 172.

the way it's done

Clipping on a Little Extra Space

A great way to increase elbow room without undue expense is to cantilever a small bay or alcove from the existing structure of the house, thereby adding a pocket of space to a room without having to build a new foundation. A wall is opened up, as if for a new window or door, but instead of adding a flat window or door frame, a framed box is "clipped" on, usually by tying its floor joists to the existing floor joists. In the photos below, you can see how a window seat was cantilevered from what had been the end of an upstairs hallway.

Separate but connected The yellow wall between the dining room and eating area and the pale green and white wall between the family room and kitchen are variations on a theme. Both walls partially divide two rooms, limiting views and access but maintaining a spatial connection.

are the crown molding running along the top of the walls—a two-piece affair consisting of blond maple and dark cherry—and the baseboard, a thick band of cherry with a beveled cherry cap that juts out a touch, giving ample weight to the bottom of the walls.

With respect to defining versus confining, the openings are a bit ambiguous, in an entirely successful way. The primary openings between the main rooms are around 4 ft. 6 in. wide, an ideal width for creating a strong connection between adjacent rooms while maintaining each room's integrity as a separate space.

Ultimately, each room has its own identity.

The most distinctive room is the dining room, which gains a suitable degree of formality not by being the most elaborate room but by being the most differentiated. Its position, sandwiched between the living room, eating area, and family room with just one exterior wall, could have condemned it to feel like leftover space. Instead, it's arguably the most visually arresting room in the house. Where the other main rooms are painted a pale green, the dining room is a rich yellow. The other rooms retain the original flat ceilings, but in the dining room the ceiling has been arched and paneled in cherry. The dining-room ceiling, like all the ceilings in this house, is a standard 8 ft. high, but there's still room for a curve, slight enough to ensure sufficient headroom, deep enough to make an impact.

A Simple Rail for Plates or Pictures

People ask me all the time how to make a plate rail like the one I have in my house. The photo at left shows one that's equally straightforward. The typical soffit built above the upper cabinets becomes a wood rail that the pictures or plates rest on. The rail is simply a piece of plywood faced with trim to create a lip. The continuation of the soffit and trim above both the cabinets and the display area keeps the look crisp, as does maintaining the same width for both the plate rail and bottom rail of the cabinet face.

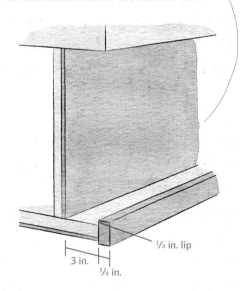

¼ in. lip

3 in.

¾ in.

Eating area   In the eating area off the kitchen, details for display (the picture rail and the wall for children's art), for storage (the cabinets and shelves), and for privacy (the sliding interior windows) come together to create a cozy feel and an intimate scale, perfect for a kids' meal or perhaps a board game with the whole family.

A single running >> line of trim elegantly emphasizes the horizontal.

The interplay of color, texture, and light generates a quiet energy.

^^
A wall longer than the room itself appears to extend space outward.

This suburban ranch was remodeled to emphasize light, color, texture, and openness.

The Illusion of More Space

Looking at this house in Bethesda, Maryland, you'd never guess it was once a typical suburban ranch house from the 1950s, contemporary in its approach to one-story living but otherwise low-slung, dimly lit, and unremarkable. When the owners sat down to work with architect Mark McInturff, they expressed a modest goal: Honor the original intent of the house but open it up and strengthen the connection between the interior and the patio, which the couple and their two children already used as an outdoor room.

What is striking about the house now is the play of natural light, the radiance and texture of brightly lit stucco, the crispness of the wall and trim colors, and especially the flow of space. The original house, in spite of its many windows and glass doors, seemed to trap space and hold it tight; it felt dark and cramped. The remodeled house feels considerably larger and more open, even though only a small family room was added. The changes Mark introduced have allowed space to move more easily from room

outside the house

Floating corner You read the yellow stucco wall in the family room as a plane around which space flows, not as a wall that defines the corner of the room. The low retaining wall outside feels more like the edge of the room than do the windows; in effect, space continues from inside to outside, and the room expands beyond its walls.

to room and from inside to outside, creating the illusion that the house contains more space.

Lighter surfaces help the house feel more open, as does daylight streaming in from skylights and clerestory windows above the rooms. But the really big change is in the way certain key walls have been treated. Let's look first at the most important wall in the house: the yellow stucco wall (see the photo on p. 174). This central spine divides the more public dining room and living room from the more private kitchen, breakfast area, and family room. The yellow wall begins at the front, carries through the original width of the house, and continues past the family-room addition, ending outside at the far corner of the backyard patio. With this wall, Mark has introduced a detail that's larger—and more dramatic—than any room in the house. Wherever you are in the main living spaces, as your eye follows the yellow wall along its considerable length, you experience a feeling of expansiveness.

The impact of the wall is only partly the result of its length.

The wall has also been given visual importance by the way it's been detailed: by its distinctive shape, material, color, texture, and trim. The regular walls of the house, whether new or old, are 2x4 studs clad in drywall, painted white. The central spine is 12 in. thick, made from plywood over

Line and Color

The crisp look of the dining room is achieved not with lavish detail but with attention to line and color. The copper trim line above the stucco wall and the thin metal window mullions are highlighted with bold colors. The rear wall of the room—just plain drywall—is accented by being painted dark gray, a suitable backdrop for bringing out the lines of the furniture. The stucco was colored before it was applied; integrally colored stucco dries with subtle changes in value not achievable by painting the stucco after it's been applied.

Details that repeat A subtle repetition of rectangular planes lends the kitchen a sense of balance and order. The refrigerator door echoes the window, the tabletop echoes the window seat, and the skylight echoes the stainless-steel backsplash behind the stove. The forms reinforce each other but never overwhelm; their unity creates a feeling of calm.

WHERE A WALL MEETS THE CEILING One of the most important details in this house is the green copper trim line that carries around the top of each stucco wall. The bright line emphasizes the overall horizontality of the house and the importance of crisp lines to the sleek feel of the interior. The color of the line and its slight indentation from the wall surface also differentiate the stucco walls from the ceiling. Working in tandem with the colored stucco, the green line makes the thick walls much more expressive than they would be if they were white.

2x10 studs, finished with stucco and painted pale yellow. The yellow stucco wall has no base trim, just a slim gap—what architects call a "reveal"—between itself and the floor, which allows you to feel the weight of the wall rather than the weight of the trim. Gaps in the wall further emphasize its thickness and heft. The top of the wall is recessed slightly and trimmed in bright-green copper. The indentation and the copper line separate the wall from the ceiling, allowing you to read the wall as a distinct and separate object.

Because it continues outside, the yellow stucco wall had to be made from materials that can withstand weather. Stone or brick would have worked, but stucco was versatile and within budget and looked just right. The copper trim is also an outdoor material. Having a wall on the inside that's made from exterior wall materials further strengthens the indoor-outdoor connection and the illusion that space continues beyond the strict boundaries of the house.

Other thickened stucco walls work in concert with the yellow wall. A light gray wall defines the front entry and one side of the dining room, and, outside, a charcoal gray stucco retaining wall defines the patio and slips past the family room, suggesting that the room really ends at this low wall, beyond the floor-to-ceiling windows. The stucco walls unify the look of the

Breakfast area

Sometimes restraint and a can of paint are all that's required. In the breakfast area, the original ceiling, paneled in cheap-looking dark wood, has been painted a bright apple green. The cheery color and the low height of the ceiling define the area as a small, intimate space apart from the taller family room and the more functional kitchen.

house and create a larger three-dimensional effect that complements the sculptural qualities of each individual wall.

The delicately colored, textured walls are also perfectly suited to capturing and reflecting light from above. In the family room, northern light enters through a tall clerestory window in the vaulted ceiling, illuminating the yellow wall on either side of the sliding glass doors below the clerestory. In the dining room, a skylight spills light onto the gray wall and the yellow wall that bookend the space, washing them with even light or hitting them with a dazzling beam, depending on the time of day and season. The endless play of light, even on cloudy days, generates a quiet kind of energy within the walls of this simple home that more than makes up for relatively low ceilings and modest square footage.

the way it's done

Window Minimalism

One hallmark of modernism is the window that isn't there, or at least that tries not to be. When the expression of a window is minimal, you look past the window. Instead of focusing on window trim and the view it frames, you experience the immediacy of the outdoors. The illustration at left shows how the window sill has been hidden by drywall.

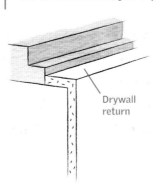

Drywall return

A composition of thoughtful details The original entry area has been given a crisp look with a few simple design moves. Sandblasting the glass door but leaving its wide sidelight clear provides some visual privacy and two distinctly contrasting qualities of light. A niche cut into the gray stucco wall reinforces the thick feel of the wall. The wall's thickness is further emphasized by a narrow gap, which also gives visitors an anticipatory glimpse into the dining room.

Signaling the entry The green ceiling juts into the living room, signaling the importance of the entry and tying the ceiling to the rest of the interior. The ceiling feels almost like one of the thick stucco walls turned on its side.

Amplifying the impact of light Two very deliberate details transform the way natural light enters and illuminates the dining room. One detail is the hole cut into the horizontal ceiling plane, which partially diffuses light from the skylight in the sloped roof above. The second detail is a window that's flush with the surface of the stucco wall. As you can see, this allows direct sunlight to enter through the south-facing window and strike the textured wall, filling the room with soft light.

Achieving balance Although the kitchen is not strictly symmetrical, it feels balanced. This is largely the result of balancing the apparent weight of things on either side of the room. For instance, the yellow stucco wall and the group of three windows have roughly the same visual weight. The room also feels balanced because the powerful combination of the built-in refrigerator and the skylight keeps pulling your eye back to the center of the space.

Sometimes the best reason for an unexpected detail is delight.
∨∨

A change of materials >> often signals a change from one space to another.

A small space feels even more intimate beside a larger space.

This house has a quality that's hard to define but easy to recognize: charm.

Creating Coziness in a Large Cottage

When the owners built their year-round house on White Bear Lake, within the St. Paul, Minnesota, city limits, they wanted it to feel like one of the easygoing lake cottages that Minnesotans have repaired to for summers and on weekends for generations. Still, with three children, they needed a fair amount of space. Architect Tom Ellison designed a cottage home that gave the family the space it required as well as warmth and coziness. At over 4,000 sq. ft., the house is a not-so-small Not So Big House, but it masterfully achieves the casual qualities and domestic scale of a much smaller cottage or cabin.

The informality apparent on the inside of the house begins with three design ideas that initially seem to have more to do with the exterior than the interior. In fact, these big moves set up the interior details for success. First, in keeping with the lake cottage tradition, Tom designed the house to appear as a one-story dwelling; the bedrooms upstairs are within the volume of the roof. This gives the

outside the house

183

WINDOW MUNTINS HELP US JUDGE SCALE This snug sitting area is actually a stair landing. Besides minimal floor area, many details contribute to its diminutive scale, some built in, like the wainscoting, some not, like the books. The muntins that divide the upper window sash into panes mark increments that relate to our hands. Take away the muntins (and the curtains), and the space loses scale and intimacy to the big outdoors.

house a cottage look outside, but it also gives the bedrooms a sheltered quality, enhanced by dormers, alcoves, and nooks under the eaves of the sweeping roof. Second, Tom did not attempt to give each room a grand view; this allows for a variety of spaces within the house, some with expansive views of the lake, some with intimate views into adjacent spaces. Finally, Tom gave the house a casual "massing," bringing together smaller house forms and roofs so it looks as though there may have been additions to the house over time.

The human scale of the individual details makes

this house feel like a home, but the details wouldn't be nearly as effective without the attention Tom paid to the scale of the house overall. Without overarching design moves like the ones Tom used, the sheer size of a larger

Entry A lowered ceiling and wood trim create a welcoming and intimately scaled entryway into a house that soon opens up to a big view. Within the entry, you have a chance to pause upon arriving before taking in the whole house.

Quality without formality

Where its traditional styling makes sense, bead board, sometimes called matchstick paneling, has qualities of scale and detail perfectly suited to a Not So Big House. The fir bead board in this hallway adds warmth and texture while maintaining a relaxed, cottage-like feel.

Master bedroom alcove The framed opening and the dark wood set this alcove apart from the rest of the master bedroom, while the small square windows lend it intimacy. The tall double-hung windows in the main space of the room soak in the view. In contrast, the low window in the alcove offers a private glimpse available only to someone sitting in the leather chairs.

An Understanding of Craft Comes First

The charm of this child's bed alcove comes from its compact size and also from the way it's been shaped and constructed, almost as though it were a piece of furniture. To get this level of detail, you need an architect who understands materials, tools, and how things fit together, and who can communicate with the craftspeople who execute the design. Or you need a craftsperson who understands design. Although there's room for spur-of-the-moment ideas, like embedding a purple marble into the trimwork, quality craftsmanship doesn't just happen—it has to be planned.

Stairs to study tower This stairway from the second floor to a study tower is a good example of useful beauty. There's only room in the tower for a writing table and a chair, so the stairway functions as the rest of the office, housing books, papers, and supplies.

house often works against attempts to add small details; the rooms end up as big, decorated boxes, not visually complex yet humanly scaled rooms.

Tom employs another concept—what he calls "counterpoint"—at many levels of detail. The light and airy living room has as its counterpoint an inglenook with lower ceilings and a much warmer, cozier feel (see the photo on p. 182). Within the inglenook, an oval window is a bright counterpoint to the stone floor, wood walls, and copper fireplace hood. The same oval window, because of its unique shape and singular position, serves as a counterpoint to the row of double-hung windows in the living room. In turn, the double-hung windows and surrounding trim are a warm, natural fir color, with fir wainscoting below, in counterpoint to the transom windows above, which are painted white, as is the wide trim band and the ceiling.

Living room The open but comfortable feel of the living room—and the details that create it—has been carefully thought through by the architect. Painting the upper third of the room white and leaving the lower two-thirds natural wood brings down the apparent height of the space and emphasizes the view through the lower windows.

Counterpoint creates variety, complexity, richness of detail.

You understand one material or color not by itself but in relation to another. Rooms and elements within rooms are not duplicates of each other but rather variations on a theme. The idea that everything doesn't have to be identical is very liberating, and it works so long as the materials, colors, and details are broadly related. The eclectic attitude of the house itself enables the owners to take a mix-and-match approach to furnishing, which, in concert with the relaxed materials and details built into the house itself, contributes to the cottage feel.

Variations on a theme The coffered ceilings in the kitchen (right) and in the living room (left) are clearly related, yet the built-up moldings that thicken and embellish the beams are different in each room. In the more formal living room, the molding has a deep, graceful curve to it; in the less formal kitchen, the molding has a narrow, more ordinary cove.

Wide sill above a sink The materials in the sink bay—slate countertop, crisply painted wood cabinets, bead-board backsplash, natural fir windows—have a sense of quality and craftsmanship but not of formality. The sill is simply an 11½-in.-wide piece of fir, supported by curved brackets, the sort of detail that could be worked into almost any kitchen to give the look of a bay window and the usefulness of a shelf.

A seemingly accidental alcove In keeping with the informality of the kitchen, the cooking alcove feels as though it could be space borrowed from a former closet or a bump-out added later. The trim framing the opening sets the alcove apart from the main space of the kitchen and accentuates the thickness of the opening, as though to build the alcove an exterior wall had to be breached. The effect is enhanced by the stained-glass windows and the spice rack, which disappear above the framed opening, creating a pleasant catch-as-catch-can appearance.

The straight grain of natural fir, the patina of stained concrete: Who needs gold?

When everything else in a space is dialed back, light comes to the fore. >>

There's ample room inside a simple house for what's inside you to be felt.

Japanese elements create a home that's as beautiful as it is serene.

Zen Warmth

At the heart of Zen Buddhism is the idea of emptiness. Properly understood, the Zen notion of emptiness, far from being chilly, is in fact radiant. It's a concept that suggests that an interior space can be plain and still be warm. In the *Tao te Ching*, the ancient Chinese sage Lao Tzu extols emptiness in a seemingly less metaphysical, more pragmatic way:

We pierce doors and windows to make a house;
And it is on these spaces where there is nothing that the
      usefulness of the house depends.
Therefore just as we take advantage of what is, we should
      recognize the usefulness of what is not.

But you don't have to embrace Eastern philosophy to appreciate the qualities of extreme simplicity in the 1,160-sq.-ft., one-story house architect Fiona O'Neill designed for herself on a coastal hillside in the Sea Ranch in northern California.

outside the house

Flush media cabinet The flush built-in media cabinet maintains visual calm by hiding clutter and also through its crisp lines. In this house, lines themselves take the place of trim, as does the thin gap between the cabinet doors or the equally thin gap between the drywall and the wood ceiling band, a slim gap the architect fondly calls a "spider crack."

Fiona's small house is an elegant blend of no-nonsense Western barn on the outside and pared-down Japanese house on the inside. Like the traditional Japanese house, Fiona's house is essentially one room, divided from time to time into smaller areas by the movable shojis. The house is also Japanese at an even deeper level: Its small, plain space exemplifies the Japanese notion of *wabi*, or "calm simplicity."

Fiona admires Japanese architecture and design for its elegance, serene quality, and deep respect for materials. All three are evident in even the smallest aspects of the house. Consider the materials themselves: clear-stained, vertical-grained Douglas fir; poured concrete with a trowel finish and an acid wash; drywall painted a buttery hue; bronze

Bedroom closet Closets to either side of the bed (along with a lowered ceiling) form a cozy alcove. Similarly, twin closets create a thickened opening between the master bedroom and bath. Shoji panels slide to conceal the closets or close off the bath. Each closet or shoji is a single element that does many things, the essence of simplicity.

---

the way it's done

Shoji for the 21st Century

These shoji screens, which were built by a local cabinetmaker, have a traditional look as well as a few contemporary touches.

The translucent panels (called *kinwashi*) are rice paper laminated to mylar for strength and water resistance.

The fir frames have wheels inside the bottom rail. The wheels travel in grooves cut into a cherry plank set within the concrete floor.

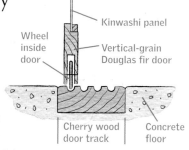

Kinwashi panel

Wheel inside door

Vertical-grain Douglas fir door

Cherry wood door track

Concrete floor

Kitchen This carefully composed kitchen emphasizes the line where one material meets another: Wood meets drywall; slate tile meets wood; stainless steel meets slate tile. A skylight placed flush with the wall enables the wall to become a reflector, setting up yet another line, where raking light strikes the cabinets and countertop.

Making the Most of Wall Thickness

Here's a detail you can adapt to almost any existing wall. The narrow wood shelves and the rich red accent color behind them have turned the slim space within this otherwise ordinary wall into storage and display area. The barn door between the living room and master bedroom plays a dual role, closing off the doorway or concealing the shelves.

anodized aluminum windows. None of these is extravagant, though each is handled with great care.

Look closely at the framed window in the solid wall at the center of the main space (seen obliquely in the photo on p. 190 and straight on in the photo at right). The wall is set a couple of feet into the space, emphasizing its solidity in contrast to the triple sliding glass doors at either side. The undivided and unadorned window captures a framed view of the trees beyond. Architects call such a glimpsed view a "Zen view," for the story of a Buddhist monk whose only view of the distant ocean was through a narrow slit in the stone wall of the courtyard beyond his house. Of course, in Fiona's house, there's more of the view through the glass doors, but the Zen view still has impact, especially because it's in line with the entry door at the opposite side of the main space. Rather than stepping into the house and confronting a long, uninterrupted wall of glass, you first take in the solid wall, the calming arrangement of egg-shaped stones, and the alluring Zen view.

Besides Japanese aesthetics, there was another consideration Fiona had to take into account: cost. Quite simply, she had a very limited budget. Many people mistakenly think the more you spend on materials, the more beauty you will have. Often, the opposite is true. In fact, if you design and build with integrity and respect, you can achieve beauty whether your materials cost $2 or $50 per sq. ft.

Kitchen counter detail   This tidy combination of modest materials—straight-grained fir, copper-flecked slate tiles, laminate countertop—shows that the effect of the whole can be more than the sum of its parts, and that a few distinctive materials (wood and tile) can elevate an ordinary one (the laminate).

The flexible use of limited space Shoji screens or similar sliding translucent panels make perfect sense in a Not So Big House, where space is limited and often must be used in more ways than one. In this house, the four shoji panels between the living room and the adjacent study greatly affect one's perception of space depending on how they are positioned. The shoji screens, handsome in their own right, also serve as the dominant decorative element of the interior.

Four panels fully closed With the panels closed, the spaces to either side each become smaller and more intimate. Light flows through the panels, yet even with the shoji closed, there is very little acoustical privacy.

Two panels slightly open The slim opening provides a sense of space beyond while maintaining a clear separation between the rooms, much like a narrow doorway.

One panel at the center With a single panel at the center of the two spaces, you perceive the study area to the left of the panel as an area distinct from the open area to the right, and you get only a hint of the bay window. In turn, the privacy of the window seat is preserved.

Four panels to one side With the panels staggered on the right side, space flows freely, but you still sense there are two rooms. The more private area leading into the guest bathroom is blocked by panels; your eye gravitates naturally toward the desk to the left.

A line of trim helps >> anchor art and other items placed on the wall.

A stairway can be a stage for displaying things, not just a bunch of steps.

Even in a mostly >> horizontal house, certain details should be vertical.

A variety of ceiling effects combine to define and differentiate space.

Ceilings Shine in Rooms without Walls

Ed and Maureen raised their children in an urbane, exquisitely crafted Prairie School home designed by architect William Purcell in Minneapolis in 1911. When they hired Susanka Studios to design their retirement home in Stowe, Vermont, they wanted the same open feeling of their old house but in a more straightforward design suited to their simpler lives and the Vermont countryside. As empty-nesters, they required a much less formal floor plan, with only spaces they would use every day—they didn't even need a formal dining room. Ed and Maureen wanted lots of natural light, views to the surrounding farmland and mountains, and places here and there made expressly for displaying their favorite antiques and artwork. Above all, though, they wanted a feeling of openness.

Even in a house with a high degree of openness, it's important to give each activity area some spatial definition. In an open house, there are few walls to accomplish this task, so I turn to the ceiling plane. Because it's relatively easy for a builder to lower sections of ceiling from the

outside the house

Kitchen cabinet close-up Placing the kitchen window flush with the cabinetry allows natural light to wash across the glass cabinet doors, making this side of the kitchen brighter.

structural joists above, I start with an 8-ft. or 9-ft. ceiling, then drop soffits, ceiling sections, or lattice to define the spaces.

In this house, I used three strategies— dropped soffits, floating lattice panels, and lowered ceilings—to modulate the actual or apparent height of the spaces. Although you aren't consciously aware of how the ceiling details affect your sense of space, they have significant impact at a subliminal level. Your eye notices changes in height and subtly recognizes the distinction between one space and another. For instance, in the short hall connecting the living room and master bedroom, I lowered the entire ceiling (see the photo on p. 202). Stepping under the low ceiling of this relatively narrow space creates a feeling of compression after the full height of the living room, as though you're moving through a tunnel. There's a subtle sense of release when you again reach full ceiling height in the master bedroom.

The key to keeping the various ceiling details from seeming like a hodgepodge is to have something tangible to which their height is keyed. In this house, the key is a continuous horizontal trim line—simply a 1x3 piece of maple, or occasionally cherry—that runs throughout the house just above the top trim of the windows. (I set the continuous trim line to the tallest item to be trimmed, the built-in refrigerator; the windows followed from there, suitably high for Ed, who is tall.) Wherever there's a soffit,

Kitchen In the kitchen, the cherry window trim becomes the top trim of the upper cabinets, neatly filling the gap between the cabinets and the dropped soffit. The soffit is set to the main trim line, which you can see continuing into the dining room in the foreground.

Shelter around an Activity

A soffit dropped below the main trim line helps define and shelter the sink, countertop, and cooking range work areas. A dropped soffit is also an ideal place to locate task lighting. The floating cherry lattice is aligned with the maple trim but serves a different purpose from the soffit, in this case defining the kitchen space and separating it slightly from the dining area.

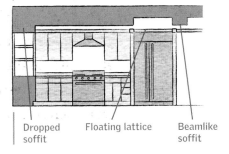

Dropped soffit   Floating lattice   Beamlike soffit

whether over a window seat, a kitchen counter, or a display shelf, it's set to the height of the trim line. The lattice panels are similarly set to the trim line.

The architectural details built into the house are important, of course, but so are the things we own. Fittingly, elements like soffits, nooks, deep shelves, and even staircases can provide a place for our favorite belongings at the same time as they embellish the spaces we live in. A handful of Ed and Maureen's favorite antiques are gathered together in the "away room," my term for a small, quiet space set apart from the more open and lively rest of the house. The away room (in this house it's essentially a sitting parlor) is tucked behind the hearth, which it shares with the living room; in the photo on pp. 206–207, you can see the away room peeking through the display shelves and the two-sided fireplace.

Other places for the display of cherished antiques, collectibles, and art objects include shelves by the hearth and a deep nook in the short hall between the entry and living room; the nook provides a place for an artful floor chest and shelves of Maureen's mother's china. By spreading out the lower stairs and dropping a soffit

Hall to master bedroom The entire ceiling in the hall to the master bedroom has been lowered to the height of the continuous trim line, so you feel a sense of compression between the full height of the living room and the full height of the bedroom. A glass door to a covered terrace and light from the window seat in the bedroom keep the hall from feeling cramped.

Master bedroom   A snug window seat in the master bedroom looks out to a small, private meadow. As with other window seats and nooks in the house, the ceiling above has been lowered to just above the window trim, increasing the cozy feel.

Laundry room   In the laundry room, a soffit is dropped below the horizontal trim line that runs through the house, providing a sense of shelter above the countertops. Without the soffit and trim, the space would feel like a narrow slot instead of a room.

the way it's done

A Simple Floating Lattice

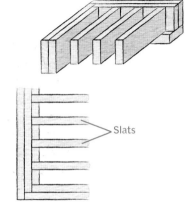

I'm often asked how to make the floating lattices I've used in several houses I've designed. The lattice in this house is made from slats of 1x3-in. solid cherry, spaced 2 in. apart. A narrow ledger strip has been added to the bottom of the long 1x3 rails, making them a little deeper than the slats. The slats are attached to the rails with screws; the ledge is there more to create clean-looking joints than to support the slats. The entire lattice is attached with metal anchor rods. Light from ceiling fixtures above the lattice is able to filter through; there are no lights in the lattice itself.

Rails

Slats

A window seat at the entry When framing a window within a window seat, it's almost always better to carry the trim fully to the top and sides of the nook, even if it means widening the trim. Otherwise, there will be an odd strip of wall (always difficult to paint) between the trim and the ceiling or sides.

over them, I created a lighted stage for a Navajo rug and a Northwest Coast bentwood cedar box (see the photo on p. 198).

The focus of this book is on the inside of houses, but we have to take a quick detour outside, because I designed Ed and Maureen's sun porch as a true room, with variations in ceiling height similar to those in the main spaces of the house. The barrel-vaulted ceiling at the center of the porch focuses attention on the nearby mountains. Flanking either side of the sweeping vault are lower flat ceilings, treated very much like the dropped soffits inside. These flat planes give a sense of shelter to a dining area on one side and a sitting area on the other. Maureen likes to say that no matter where you sit in her home, there's something good to look at. That's true, I hope, whether you're on the sun porch looking out at Mount Mansfield or in the away room looking at the small Hudson River valley landscape painting over the hearth.

picture this

SIZING A VANITY MIRROR
Whether it's framed or just a sheet of glass, a large mirror looks much better above a vanity if it takes up the entire wall, from one side to the other and from the vanity top to the ceiling. A mirror that's not large enough to fill the wall leaves awkward spaces around it that never feel quite right.

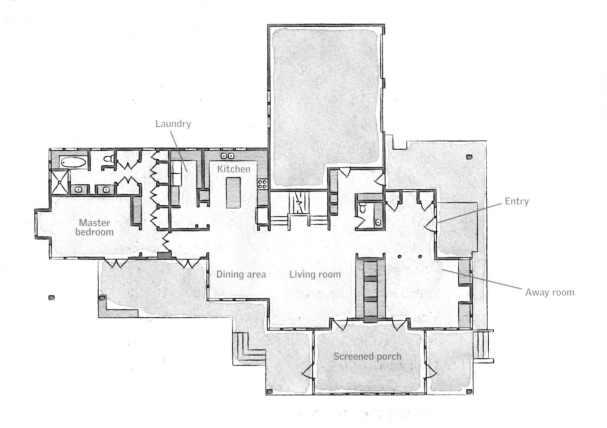

Laundry

Kitchen

Entry

Master
bedroom

Dining area   Living room

Away room

Screened porch

Master bath In the master bath, the ceiling is lowered to the window trim line. The trim ties the glass shower stall to the rest of the space and gives it more substance. Wood is okay in a shower as long as it's protected (this trim has a urethane finish) and out of the direct line of water.

Ceilings Shine in Rooms without Walls   **205**

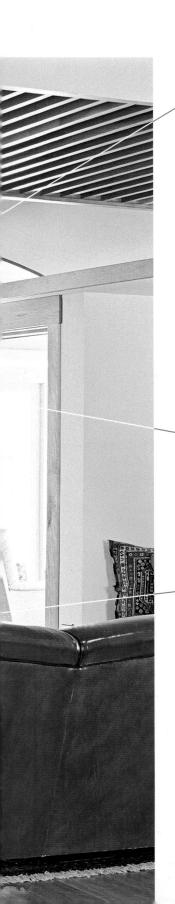

A shared approach to trim connects living room and porch The sun porch maintains the trim line of the living room, but in this casual outdoor room, the trim is painted white and the dropped soffit, like the ceiling, is paneled in bead board. The cove above the trim line houses lights that illuminate the curved ceiling at night. The plane of the soffit continues beyond the screened windows to become the wide eaves of the roof.

Of trim lines and soffits This corner of the away room (on the other side of the hearth from the living room) mirrors the living room with a similar door and a crescent window to the sun porch. The continuous trim line lends order to what's happening both above and below it. Above the line, the crescent window springs from the trim and a boxed area over the display shelf houses a stereo speaker. Below the trim line, as in the living room, there's a dropped soffit. The soffit defines a deep display shelf and the hearth but continues just a few inches wide over the door to bring down the apparent height of the away room.

A virtual hallway It's easy to see the floating cherry lattice that helps divide the dining area from the living room. You have to look more closely to notice the beamlike soffit above the lattice (running perpendicular to it) that even more subtly defines a pathway through the living room, a kind of virtual hallway connecting the entry to the master bedroom. Look again at the photo on the facing page and you'll see this narrow soffit defining the pathway back toward the entry.

Architects and Designers

David Linzee Amory, AIA
Amory Architects
7 Harvard Square
Brookline, MA 02445
(617) 277-4111
www.amoryarchitects.com

Kevin deFreitas Architects
885 Albion Street
San Diego, CA 92106
(619) 235-8858
www.defreitasarchitects.com

James Estes, FAIA
Estes/Twombly Architects, Inc.
79 Thames Street
Newport, RI 02840
(401) 846-3336
www.estestwombly.com

Curves and Color
Bring a Tiny House
to Life
pp. 18–25

A Spare House
that Sparkles
pp. 76–83

Classic Cottage
Simplicity
pp. 42–49

Barry D. Burgess
Insite Northwest, LLC
2339 Fairview Avenue, Suite N
Seattle, WA 98102
(206) 324-8473

Gail A. Douglass, AIA, and Thomas R. Utley
2853 Ontario Road NW #202
Washington, DC 20009
(202) 234-1964

Tina Govan
Tina Govan Architect
513 Holden Street
Raleigh, NC 27604
(919) 890-4124
www.tinagovan.com

A Houseboat
Full of Nautical Charm
pp. 84–91

Grace, Elegance, and
Storage—in 650 sq. ft.
pp. 158–165

Serenity
on a Budget
pp. 26–33

CTA Design Builders, Inc.
Architects and General Contractors
Julie Campbell, AIA, and Buzz Tenenbom, AIA
2556 11th Avenue West
Seattle, WA 98119
(206) 286-1692
www.ctabuilds.com

Tom Ellison and Leffert Tigelaar
TEA2 Architects
2724 West 43rd Street
Minneapolis, MN 55410
(612) 929-2800
www.tea2architects.com

Jane Kuelbs and Bruce Rogers
Kuelbs + Rogers, Ltd.
1421 Leonard Place
Evanston, IL 60201
(847) 328-2597
www.kplusrdesign.com

The Nature
of Materials
pp. 142–149

Creating Coziness
in a Large Cottage
pp. 182–189

Defining Space
with Light
pp. 92–99

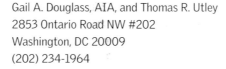

Jean Rehkamp Larson, AIA,
Mark Larson, AIA, Keith Kamman,
and Susan Nackers Ludwig
Rehkamp Larson Architects, Inc.
2732 West 43rd Street
Minneapolis, MN 55410
(612) 285-7275
www.rehkamplarson.com

Rooms Defined
but Not Confined
pp. 166–173

Fiona E. O'Neill, Architect
P.O. Box 108
The Sea Ranch, CA 95497
(707) 785-0040

Zen Warmth
pp. 190–197

Jim Samsel, AIA, (principal)
and Nathan Bryant (designer)
Samsel Architects, PA
60 Biltmore Avenue
Asheville, NC 28801
(828) 253-1124
www.samselarchitects.com

Simple Trim,
Substantial Impact
pp. 150–157

Mark McInturff, FAIA
McInturff Architects
4220 Leeward Place
Bethesda, MD 20816
(301) 229-3705
www.mcinturffarchitects.com

The Illusion
of More Space
pp. 174–181

Gitta Robinson and Richard Grisaru
Robinson + Grisaru Architecture PC
55 Washington Street, Suite 711
Brooklyn, NY 11201
(718) 923-0040
www.rgarch.com

Rooms Afloat
above a Garden
pp. 124–133

James Strickland (design principal),
Benjamin Showalter, and Jerry Sommer
Historical Concepts, LLC
430 Prime Point, Suite 103
Peachtree City, GA 30269
(770) 487-8041
www.historicalconcepts.com

Laid-Back
Florida Cracker
pp. 100–107

Frederick Noyes, FAIA
Frederick Noyes • Architects
(formerly Modigliani/Noyes Architects)
129 Kingston Street
Boston, MA 02111
(617) 451-1962

Order in the Details
pp. 68–75

Stephen Robinson Architect
2218 Lebaron Drive
Atlanta, GA 30345
(404) 636-5939

A Modest Ranch
Opens Up
pp. 134–141

Sarah Susanka, FAIA
www.susanka.com

Ceilings Shine
in Rooms without Walls
pp. 198–207

Douglas Teiger
Abramson Teiger Architects
8924 Lindblade Street
Culver City, CA 90035
(310) 838-8998
www.abramsonteiger.com

Reinventing
the Family Home
pp. 34–41

Jamie Wolf
Wolfworks, Inc.
195 West Main Street
Avon, CT 06001
(860) 676-9238
www.homesthatfit.com

A Jewel Box
of Texture and Detail
pp. 50–59

Stephen Zagorski, AIA
Stephen Zagorski Architects
P.O. Box 50196
Austin, TX 78763
(512) 789-3259
(512) 472-5156
www.stevezagorski.com

Texas Tuscan
pp. 60–67

Peter Twombly, AIA
Estes/Twombly Architects, Inc.
79 Thames Street
Newport, RI 02840
(401) 846-3336
www.estestwombly.com

interior consultant: Kirby Goff
Kirby Goff Interior Architecture & Design
150 Chestnut St.
Providence, RI 02903
(401) 490-5929

Detailed
for the View
pp. 108–115

Gail Wong and John Koppe
Gail L. Wong Architects
2609 East Garfield Street
Seattle, WA 98112
(206) 325-4025
www.glwarc.com

Craftsman Character
on a Narrow Lot
pp. 116–123